**"When the going gets weird,
the weird turn pro"**

Also by Hunter S. Thompson

Hell's Angels
Fear and Loathing in Las Vegas
Fear and Loathing: On the Campaign Trail '72
The Great Shark Hunt
The Curse of Lono
Generation of Swine
Songs of the Doomed
Screwjack
The Proud Highway
The Rum Diary
Kingdom of Fear

BETTER
THAN
SEX
CONFESSIONS OF A POLITICAL JUNKIE
Gonzo Papers Vol. 4

BETTER THAN SEX

CONFESSIONS OF A POLITICAL JUNKIE

Gonzo Papers Vol. 4

Hunter S. Thompson

THE RANDOM HOUSE PUBLISHING GROUP • NEW YORK

A Ballantine Book
Published by The Random House Publishing Group

Published in the United States by Ballantine Books, an imprint of The Random House Publishing Group, a division of Random House, Inc., New York, and simultaneously in Canada by Random House of Canada Limited, Toronto.

BALLANTINE and colophon are registered trademarks of Random House, Inc.

A portion of this book was originally published in *Rolling Stone.*

Grateful acknowledgment is made to *The New York Times* for permission to reprint " 'Freak Power' Candidate May Be Next Sheriff in Placid Aspen" by Anthony Ripley (10/13/70). Copyright © 1970 by The New York Times Company. Reprinted by permission.

Library of Congress Catalog Card Number: 95-94419

ISBN: 0-345-39635-9

Cover photo by Louie Psihoyos

www.ballantinebooks.com

Manufactured in the United States of America
First Ballantine Books Trade Paperback Edition: September 1995

19 18 17 16

To Nicole,
my vampire in the Garden of Agony

CONTENTS

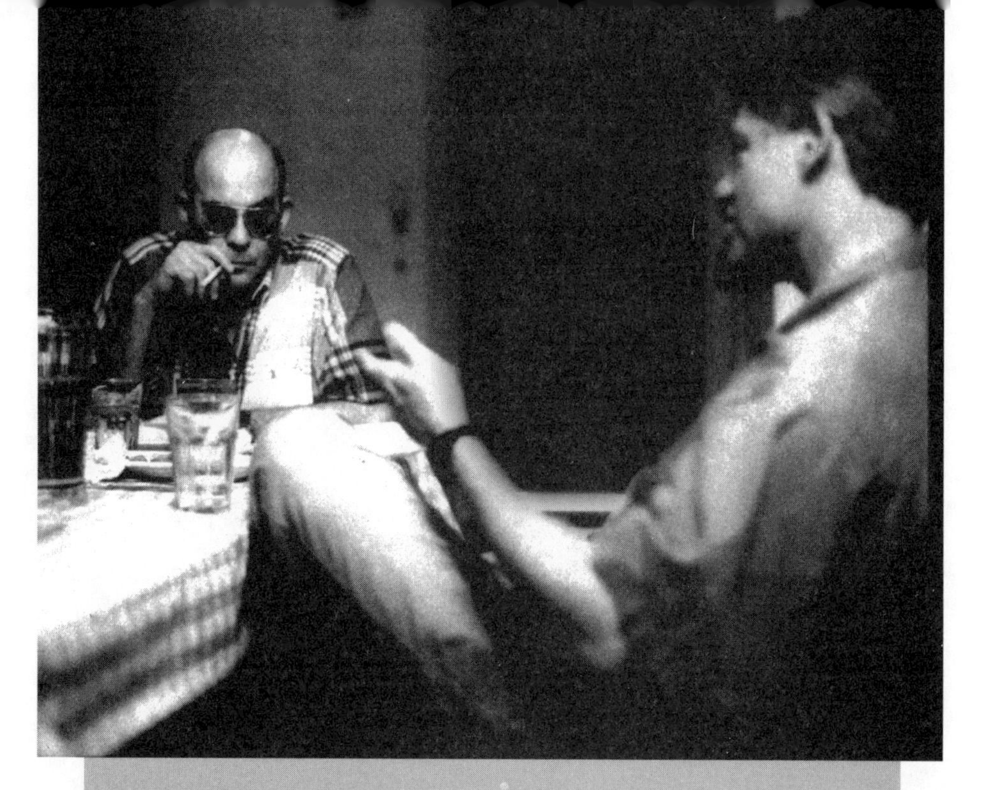

Influence peddling: Candidate Clinton bargains for the rock 'n' roll vote in the smoke-filled back room of Doe's Café, July 31, 1992

The Old Woman and the Snake

A PARABLE

An ***old woman*** *was walking down the road when she saw a gang of thugs beating a poisonous snake. She rescued the snake and carried it back to her home, where she nursed it back to health. They became friends and lived together for many months. One day they were going into town, and the old woman picked him up and the snake bit her. Repeatedly. "O God," she screamed, "I am dying! Why? I was your friend. I saved your life! I trusted you! Why did you bite me?"*

The snake looked up at her and said, "Lady, you knew I was a snake when you first picked me up."

Amendment IV

TO THE U.S. CONSTITUTION

THE RIGHT OF THE PEOPLE to be secure in their persons, houses, papers, and effects, against unreasonable searches and seizures, shall not be violated, and no warrants shall issue, but upon probable cause, supported by oath or affirmation, and particularly describing the place to be searched, and the persons or things to be seized.

The Raven

"Prophet!" said I, "thing of evil!—prophet still, if bird or devil!—

. . . .

"Take thy beak from out my heart, and take thy form from off my door!"
Quoth the Raven, "Nevermore."

And the Raven, never flitting, still is sitting, still is sitting
On the pallid bust of Pallas just above my chamber door;

. . . .

And my soul from out that shadow that lies floating on the floor
Shall be lifted—nevermore!

—Edgar Allan Poe, 1845

The Campaign Time Line beginning on page 40 is what it appears to be—a rolling calendar of real events, large and small, that tracked the 1992 presidential campaign. Life went on, and not much really changed in all those wretched little weeks. If there is no joy in Mudville tonight, the Campaign Time Line might help to explain why.

—HST

PART ONE

CHAPTER 1
AUTHOR'S NOTE

Confessions of a shootist: Cruel humor on the campaign trail, from the murder of JFK to the crimes of the Marquis de Sade

Trace a line of goose pimples up the thin young arm. Slide the needle in and push the bulb watching the junk hit him all over. Move right in with the shit and suck junk through all the hungry young cells.

—William S. Burroughs, *The Soft Machine*

JOHN F. KENNEDY, who seized the White House from Richard Nixon in a frenzied campaign that turned a whole generation of young Americans into political junkies, got shot in the head for his efforts, murdered in Dallas by some hapless geek named Oswald who worked for either Castro, the mob, Jimmy Hoffa, the CIA, his dominatrix landlady or the odious, degenerate FBI chief J. Edgar Hoover. The list is long and crazy—maybe Marilyn Monroe's first husband fired those shots from the Grassy Knoll. Who knows? A whole generation of American journalists is still embarrassed by their failure to answer that question.

JFK's ghost will haunt the corridors of power in America for as long as the grass is green and the rivers run to the sea....Take my word for it, Bubba. I have heard his footsteps for 30 years and

I still feel guilty about not being able to explain the biggest news story of my lifetime to my son.

AT ONE POINT, not long ago, I went to the desperate length of confessing to the murder myself. We were finishing breakfast in a patio restaurant on a bright Sunday morning in Boulder. It was a stylish place near the campus, where decent people could meet after pretending they had just come from church and get fashionably drunk on mimosas and white wine. The tables were separated by ferns and potted palms. Bright orange impatiens flowers drooped from hanging urns.

Even I can't explain why I said what I did. I had been up all night with my old friend Allen Ginsberg, the poet, and we had both slid into the abyss of whiskey madness and full-bore substance abuse. It was wonderful, but it left me a little giddy by the time noon rolled around.

"Son," I said, "I'm sorry to ruin your breakfast, but I think the time has finally come to tell you the truth about who killed John Kennedy."

He nodded but said nothing. I tried to keep my voice low, but emotion made it difficult.

"It was *me*," I said. "I am the one who shot Jack Kennedy."

"What?" he said, glancing quickly over his shoulder to see if others were listening. Which they were. The mention of Kennedy's name will always turn a few heads, anywhere in the world—and god only knows what a tenured Professor of American Political History might feel upon hearing some grizzled thug in a fern bar confess to his own son that he was the one who murdered John F. Kennedy. It is one of those lines that will not fall on deaf ears.

My son leaned forward and stared into my eyes as I explained the raw details and my reasons for killing the President in cold blood, many years ago. I spoke about ballistics and treachery and my "secret work for the government" in Brazil, when he thought I was in the Peace Corps in the sixties.

"I gave up killing about the time you were born," I said. "But I could never tell you about it, until now."

He nodded solemnly for a moment, then laughed at me and called for some tea. "Don't worry, Dad," he said.

"Good boy," I said. "Now we can finally be honest with each other. I feel naked and clean for the first time in 30 years."

"Not me," he said. "Now I'll have to turn you in."

"What?" I shouted. "You treacherous little bastard!" Many heads had turned to stare at us. It was a weird moment for them. The man who killed Kennedy had just confessed publicly to his son, and now they were cursing each other. Ye gods, what next?

What indeed? How warped can it be for a child born into the sixties to finally be told that his father was the hired shootist who killed Kennedy? Do you call 911? Call a priest? Or act like a cockroach and say nothing?

NO WONDER the poor bastards from Generation X have lost their sense of humor about politics. Some things are not funny to the doomed, especially when they've just elected a President with no sense of humor at all. The joke is over when even victory is a downhill run into hardship, disappointment and a queasy sense of betrayal. If you can laugh in the face of these things, you are probably ready for a staff job with a serious presidential candidate. The humor of the campaign trail is relentlessly cruel and brutal. If you think you like jokes, try hanging around the cooler after midnight with hired killers like James Carville or the late Lee Atwater, whose death by cancer in 1991 was a fatal loss to the Bush reelection effort. Atwater could say, without rancor, that he wanted to castrate Michael Dukakis and dump him on the Boston Common with his nuts stuffed down his throat. Atwater said a lot of things that made people cringe, but he usually smiled when he said them, and people tried to laugh.

It was Deep Background stuff, they figured; of *course* he didn't mean it. Hell, in some states you could go to *prison* for making treats like that. *Felony menacing*, two years minimum; *Conspiracy* to commit Murder and/or Felony Assault with Intent to commit Great Bodily Harm, minimum 50 years in Arkansas and Texas; also Kidnapping (death), Rape, Sodomy,

Malicious Disfigurement, Treason, Perjury, Gross Sexual Imposition and Aggravated Conspiracy to Commit all of the above (600 years, minimum).... And all of this without anybody ever *doing* anything. Ho, ho. How's that for the wheels of justice, Bubba? Six hundred fify-two years, just for downing a few gin-bucks at lunch and trading jokes among warriors....

> ***Richard Nixon was not a Crook. Ho, ho.***
>
> ***George Bush was innocent. Ho, ho.***
>
> ***Ed Rollins bribed every Negro preacher in New Jersey to hold down the black vote for the Governor in '93. Hee-haw.***
>
> ***James Carville set Hamilton Jordan's heart on fire and then refused to piss down his throat to save his life. Ho, ho.***

That is the kind of humor that campaign junkies admire and will tell to their children—for the same perverse reasons that make me confess to my son, over breakfast, that I blew John Kennedy's head off in Dallas.

You have to be very mean to get a laugh on the campaign trail. There is no such thing as paranoia.

NOT EVERYBODY will get a belly laugh out of these things, but if you want to get elected, it is better to be Mean than to be Funny.

Cruel jokes are a big part of life in any environment where speed freaks, work addicts and obsessive-compulsive political junkies are ripped to the tits day and night for thirteen straight months on their own adrenaline and swollen more and more each day with the kind of hubris that comes when you try to cross Innocence and Ambition all at once and you start seeing yourself on the front page of the *New York Times* in a photo with the next president getting off a jet plane in Texas or Boston or Washington, surrounded by a gang of hard-eyed U.S. Secret Service agents escorting you through the cheering crowd....

It's a rush that a lot of people will tell you is higher than any drug they've ever tried or even heard about, and maybe *better than sex*...which is a weird theory and often raises unsettling personal questions, but it is a theory nonetheless, and on some days I've even believed it myself.

But not really, and days like that are so rare that I usually can't even remember them.... But when I do, it is like a nail in my eye. The pain goes away, but the wound stays forever. The scar never quite heals over—and whenever it seems like it's going to, I pick at it. I have some scars that go back 33 years, and I still remember how they happened, just like it was yesterday.

NOT EVERYBODY is comfortable with the idea that politics is a guilty addiction. But it *is*. They *are* addicts, and they *are* guilty and they *do* lie and cheat and steal—like all junkies. And when they get in a frenzy, they will sacrifice anything and anybody to feed their cruel and stupid habit, and there *is* no cure for it. That is addictive thinking. That is politics—especially in presidential campaigns. That is when the addicts seize the high ground. They care about nothing else. They are salmon, and they must spawn. They are addicts, and so am I. The fish hear their music and I hear mine. Politics is like the Guinea Worm. It sneaks into your body and grows like a cyst from within—until finally it gets so big and strong that it bursts straight through the skin, a horrible red worm with a head like a tiny cobra, snapping around in the air as it struggles to breathe.

This is true. There are pictures of it happening, in the Encyclopedia Britannica. The Guinea Worm is real...and so is politics, for that matter. The only difference is that you can get rid of the worm by gripping its head and wrapping its body around a stick, then pulling it very slowly out of your flesh, like a bird pulls an earthworm out of the ground.

Getting rid of a political addiction is not so easy. The worm is smaller and tends to migrate upward, to the skull, where it feeds and thrives on the tissue. It is undetectable in the early stage, usually diagnosed as common "brain fluke"—which is also incurable—and by the time it gets powerful enough to bore its way through a soft spot in the skull, not even witch doctors will touch it.

The Guinea Worm problem is confined mainly to equatorial Africa, thank god. We are not ready for it in this country. A declining standard of living is one thing, but getting used to the notion that any lesion on your leg might be the first sign of a worm about to erupt is still unacceptable to the normal American. Even a single (confirmed) case of Guinea Worm in Washington would be taken as an omen and doom Bill Clinton's presidency. An epidemic would finish the Democratic party and put Pat Buchanan in the White House for 20 years.

That is a horrible scenario, Bubba, and it probably won't happen. We have enough trouble in Washington without the goddamn Guinea Worm—although many presidents have suffered from worse things, but these were always kept secret from the public.

That is the job of the Secret Service, and they are good at it. "Degenerates are our specialty," one agent joked. "We cover up things every day of the week that would embarrass the Marquis de Sade."

THE MARQUIS WAS not a pastoral man. He preferred to live in the city, where people were closer together and the fine arts flourished. The Marquis was an artist, and artists roamed free in the city...for a while, at least. It depended on what kind of artist you were, and the Marquis was one of a kind...

He had a style all his own, they said, and he hated to be interfered with. With his artist's love of life, he disdained politicians as scum. He was also a serious drinker with a keen taste for laudanum and other opiates that occasionally drove him wild and attracted unwanted attention from the local police, no matter where he lived.

They always interfered, even in Paris, and soon he came to hate them—even fear them—when he saw that they not only hated his art, they hated him, and they wanted to lock him up.

Which they did, more than once—and even when he was loose, they hounded him. By the spring of 1788 his reputation was so foul that he was often chased through the streets like a midnight rat.

His friends tried to intercede: The Marquis was, after all, a French nobleman, and also a working artist. So what if his art was a little weird? If he didn't do it, somebody else would. So leave him alone and mind your own business.

Which was not bad advice, at the time. The law enforcement in Paris had been pretty stable for most of that century, but in the final years it got strange. The police were no longer feared. Angry mobs set police stations on fire and had to be gunned down by soldiers. Nobody seemed to give a fuck.

The mood of the city was so ugly that even the Marquis de Sade became a hero of the people. On July 14, 1789, he led a mob of crazed rabble in overrunning a battalion of doomed military police defending the infamous Bastille Prison, and they swarmed in to "free all political prisoners," as the Marquis later explained.

It was the beginning of the French Revolution, and de Sade himself was said to have stabbed five or six soldiers to death as his mob stormed the prison and seized the keys to the Arsenal.* The mob found only eight "political prisoners" to free, and four of those were killed by nightfall in the savage melee over looting rights for the guns and ammunition.

AND THAT is the story, folks, of how the Marquis de Sade was finally forced into politics. They pushed him too far. So he decided to control his environment. . . . And the moral of the story is never lean on the weird. Or they will chop your head off. And perverts will eat your brains.

Take my word for it, Bubba. I am an expert on these things. I have been there.

---

* Historians have noted that one of the prisoners slain was named Rogere Clinton—a deserter from the French Foreign Legion.

ON ELECTION night in 1972, for instance, I was in Sioux Falls, South Dakota, with George and Eleanor McGovern—and Frank Mankiewicz and John Holum and Sandy Berger and Gary Hart and Barbara Shailor and Bob McNeely and Eli Segal and Carl Wagner and Rick Stearns and Bill Greider and Johnny Apple and Connie Chung and Tim Crouse and John Gage and Don Pennebaker and Julie Christie and Warren Beatty and—

(Whoops! Was Warren there? Had he jumped ship by then? Did he quit in the stretch and not show up at all in November, when the deal went down and we were all alone out there in that goddamn joyless, sexless humpbacked stupid little city that was suddenly a million miles away from the Beverly Wilshire and another grim million from the White House?

But he was not in Sioux Falls that night, unless he was hiding in some dingy penthouse on the outskirts of town. I remember every person who was there, and I can still see them frantically doing their jobs all the way to the brutal end.)

TWENTY-TWO POINTS. Try that for a bad night on the campaign trail. It was horrible. The landslide started early and never let up. Nixon won 49 states. Not even South Dakota went for McGovern. It was like being in the Alamo. We were surrounded by the armies of Nixon—even in our candidate's hometown, long before the polls closed in California, they were starting to close in like hyenas. The scent of blood was dangerously thick in the air.

McGovern

I was laying low with Frank Mankiewicz in a dark corner of the Feedlot Lounge, when the tab he'd been running for six months was abruptly "closed." . . .

No more credit. No more margaritas.

The joke was over. The dream was dead. It was like going down on the good ship *Reuben James*. About six o'clock that night, Frank got a call from the credit manager at United Airlines, wanting to talk to whoever was "in charge" of paying the bill for six months of chartered 727s and myriad smaller aircraft from the UAL Presidential Charter Fleet, at five dollars per mile, as contracted, for something like 16 million passenger-miles in all 50 states and 9,000 hours of triple-overtime pay for pilots and crew. "Who knows what they might say if they're not paid?" the man asked Frank. "They have, as I'm sure you know, been witness to many horrible and dangerous things in the course of their work and their duties while employed by this doomed and clearly ill-advised farce of a presidential campaign. Do you know how many people would go to jail for the rest of their lives, Frank? If our pilots were ever deposed? Or the stewardesses? Jesus. Some of it makes me sick, Frank, and nobody wants to talk about it, eh?

"Fuck no! So pay the goddamn bill, Frank. Or at least part of it. . .please. Just write me a check. So what if it's bad? Who cares? You write the paper, boss, and I'll hang it."

Frank was talking to the man on a boom box in the pressroom, where they'd finally tracked him down, so we all heard the threats and the ugly squeeze that came next: "No more planes for you, big boy. Not tonight and not tomorrow. You're canceled! And so is the plane back to Washington. Ho, ho. Good luck with no crew and no pilots. The bus leaves twice a day."

Which it did—but we were not on it. We took the 727, which had been topped off with premium jet fuel before noon on Election Day and charged to UAL, as always. Frank wrote the check and I signed it and we had it hand-delivered to the United credit office in Chicago by a woman they called The Sioux City Gobbler. And that was the last we heard of it.

We fled in our jet before noon, just ahead of the writ of seizure. It was getting dark when we finally taxied up to a dimly lit hangar at the far end of National Airport, just across the river from Washington, where the national staff had gathered to meet the dead and the wounded and carry them off to wherever failures get carried off to in Washington, after they get brutally beaten in public.

Another thing I still remember from that horrible day in November of '72 was that some dingbat named Clinton was said to be almost single-handedly responsible for losing 222 counties in Texas—including Waco, where he was McGovern's regional coordinator—and was "terminated without pay, *with prejudice*," and sent back home to Arkansas "with his tail between his legs," as an aide put it.

"We'll never see *that* stupid bastard again," one McGovern aide muttered. "Clinton—Bill Clinton. Yeah. Let's remember that name. He'll never work again, not in Washington."

Late-nineteenth-century people developed a powerful attitude toward drug abuse, resting on conceptions of individual worth and the national purpose. Medical, pharmaceutical, and other influential organizations understood the threats addiction posed for special groups such as women, professionals, and young people. Yet while loathing and fearing addiction, many late-nineteenth-century people sympathized with addicts. They condemned the use of drugs for escape or sensual pleasure, but many people believed that addiction was a form of physiological slavery, which alleviated the user's guilt....

—H. Wayne Morgan, *Yesterday's Addict*

O, YE OF LITTLE FAITH.... Politics is like a death march when you lose too many times, and it sure as hell isn't the losers who tell you stupid things like "Politics is better than sex." Winning is an addiction, and Bill Clinton is a pure junkie.

Most people will deny their addictions—but not me. I have an addictive personality, and medical experts agree that I can't be cured—which used to worry people running for President of the United States when I showed up with no warning at their homes late at night for random confrontations on issues of national security or regressive taxation or rumors of ugly personal scandals in the family....

But that was a long time ago, and things are different now. Once I became a registered compound-addict, there were no more problems with red tape or fears of public exposure and disgrace just for being seen with me.

No candidate will risk being linked with a "suspected" addict—but a registered, admitted addict is a whole different thing. As long as I'd confessed, I was okay. Nobody really cared about the countless criminal addictions that preyed on me day and night—just as long as I was not in denial.

That was the key. As long as they knew that I knew I was sick and guilty, I was safe. They were only trying to help me.

Look at Bill Clinton. He sent his own brother to prison "for his own good"; Bill was a New Age sensitive guy, and poor Roger was the evil dunce of the family, the black sheep kid brother who was always getting in trouble. While his brilliant big brother was shaking hands with President Kennedy in the Rose Garden, Roger was hanging out at the Toddle House in Little Rock and getting to know the local police.... And when Bill went to Oxford as a Rhodes scholar, Roger went to Memphis and got himself involved with what was then called "the criminal element." Soon he was running wild and getting his name in the newspapers. Some people said he was a dope fiend and needed to be protected, for his own good.

It was only a few years later, when the State Police came to Governor Clinton and told him the bad news—his little brother was about to be busted for drugs in a sting operation—that Bill did what he had to do. Roger was a criminal, and Bill was not—Roger went to the Big House, and Bill went to the White House.

I KNEW I HAD no choice but to be a part of the 1992 election. Even though I realized it was not going to be much fun, win or lose—except briefly for the campaign staff of the lone survivor, who would be the next president of the United States and move, with his people, to the White House, where many would drown or be bashed to death on the dark reefs of the fast lane.

The only other sector of the electorate who would feel any joy on election night were the junkies like me, who understood in their hearts that the only real priority in 1992 was beating George Bush. Nothing else mattered.

CHAPTER 2
THE BOOK OF SCREEDS

The roots of addiction: The degradation of American politics in the final years of the American Century...Abandon all hope, ye who enter here... Welcome to Mr. Bill's neighborhood: The tragic story of one man's struggle with the forces of evil and greed on the campaign trail, from Kennedy to Clinton...There is no such thing as an ex-junkie...

I have existed from the morning of the world, and I shall exist until the last star falls from the heavens.

Although I have taken the form of Gaius Caligula, I am all men, as I am no Man—and, so, I am a God.

—Bill Clinton, 1993

THERE ARE NOT MANY flat-out good political movies on the racks these days—and not many ever made, for that matter—but the handful of good ones are humdingers.

Being There is one of them, and so is *All the King's Men*. *Citizen Kane* will tell you a lot about politics, and so will *JFK* or

The Life of Richard Nixon. But if you want a serious political movie, have a long look at *Caligula*, which a lot of people will tell you is the best.

Caligula is a genuine monstrosity—a saga of greed, failure and corruption that makes Nixon seem like an amateur and Charles Manson a punk. Caligula was serious, and he had no use for journalists.

THERE ARE a lot of ways to practice the art of journalism, and one of them is to use your art like a hammer to destroy the right people—who are almost always your enemies, for one reason or another, and who usually *deserve* to be crippled because they are wrong.

This is a dangerous notion, and few professional journalists will endorse it—calling it "vengeful" and "primitive" and "perverse" regardless of how often they might do the same thing themselves. "That kind of stuff is opinion," they say, "and the reader is *cheated* if it's not *labeled* as opinion."

Well...maybe so. Maybe Tom Paine cheated his readers and Mark Twain was a devious fraud with no morals at all who used journalism for his own foul ends.... And maybe H. L. Mencken should have been locked up for trying to pass off his opinions on gullible readers as normal "objective journalism."

Mencken scorned such criticism as the jabbering of dumb yahoos—especially when it came from world-famous (U.S.) presidential candidate William Jennings Bryan, who called Mencken "a disgrace to journalism" and "so genetically twisted that he couldn't even write a straight item for the obituary page."

Unfortunately for Bryan, he died before Mencken did—and he paid a terrible price for it, when H. L. wrote his obituary in the *American Mercury*. It was, and remains, one of the most hideous things ever written about a dead man in the history of American letters, and I remember being shocked when I first read it—thinking, Ye gods, this is *evil.* I had learned in school that Bryan was a genuine hero of history, but after reading

Mencken's brutal obit, I knew in my heart that he was, in truth, a monster.

It was clearly opinion—no doubt about that—but I believed it then and I believe it now. Bryan was a dumb brute and a raving charlatan who argued desperately in court that a male is not a mammal and thought anybody who disagreed with him should go to prison. His shadow hung over the White House for decades, and he was worshiped by millions. I shudder to know that most of my friends from high school still think he was a great man.

Mencken understood that politics—as used in journalism—was the art of controlling his environment, and he made no apologies for it. In my case, using what politely might be called "advocacy journalism," I've used reporting as a weapon to affect political situations that bear down on *my* environment.

It worked for Pat Buchanan.

And it almost worked for me.

In politics there is no honor.

—Benjamin Disraeli

ON SOME DAYS you get what you deserve in the politics business, and in the autumn of 1970, I almost got mine.

I was *on the ballot* that year—the Freak Power candidate for sheriff of Pitkin County, Colorado. Somewhere around Halloween, I looked at the numbers and realized that I might actually win. A secret BBC TV poll of the community showed me running far ahead of the GOP candidate while the Democratic incumbent and I were "too close to call."

The campaign combined journalism and politics. It was necessary. We had no choice.

October 20, 1970

To whom it may concern:

Contrary to widespread rumors and a plague of wishful thinking, I am very serious about my candidacy for the office of sheriff in the coming November election. Anybody who thinks I'm kidding is a fool: 739 new registrations since the September primary is no joke in a county with a total vote of less than 3,000. So the time has come, I think, to dispense with evil humor and come to grips with the strange possibility that the next sheriff of this county might very well be a foul-mouthed outlaw journalist with some very rude notions about life-styles, law enforcement and political reality in America.

Why not? This is a weird twist in my life, and despite the natural horror of seeing myself as the main pig, I feel ready. And I think Aspen is ready: not only for a stone-freak sheriff, but for a whole new style of local government—the kind of government Thomas Jefferson had in mind when he used the word "democracy." We have not done too well with that concept—not in Aspen or anywhere else—and the proof of our failure is the wreckage of Jefferson's dream that haunts us on every side, from coast to coast, on the TV news and a thousand daily newspapers. We have blown it: that fantastic possibility that Abe Lincoln called "the last, best hope of man."

Or maybe not. Not completely, anyway. There are people who argue that we can still get a grip on ourselves, and salvage some of the pieces. But not even Nixon would be willing to bet seriously on this chance, and in fact the only thing that makes it worth trying is that we don't really have much choice. The alternatives are too ugly—for our children, if not for ourselves.

This is the grim context that our politicians have forced on us, even in Aspen. This valley is no longer a refuge or a hideout from reality. For years, that was true; this valley was the best of both worlds—an outpost of urban "culture" buried deep in the rural Rockies. It was a very saleable property, as they say in show business, and for 20 years the selling-orgy boomed fat and heavy.

And now we are reaping the whirlwind—big-city problems too malignant for small-town solutions, Chicago-style traffic in a town without stoplights, Oakland-style drug busts continually bungled by simple cowboy cops who see nothing wrong with kicking handcuffed prisoners in the ribs while the sheriff stands by watching, seeing nothing wrong with it either. While the ranchers howl about zoning, New York stockbrokers and art hustlers sell the valley out from under them. The county attorney has his own iron mine and his own industrial slum at the mouth of the valley. The county commissioners are crude dimwits, lackeys for every big-city dealer who wants a piece of the action.

This is a nightmare, a bad movie, a terrifying joke on us all. We are shitting in our own nest, and the stench is becoming intolerable. Where will it end? When? How? And who will throw the switch?

Only serious people can laugh.

—Federico Fellini

hunter
thompson

for sheriff

1970
aspen colorado

TENTATIVE PLATFORM

6 OF THE 13 POINTS

THOMPSON FOR SHERIFF...ASPEN, COLORADO, 1970

1) Sod the streets at once. Rip up all city streets with jackhammers and use the junk-asphalt (after melting) to create a huge parking and auto-storage lot on the outskirts of town—preferably somewhere out of sight, like between the new sewage plant and McBride's new shopping center. All refuse and other garbage could be centralized in this area—in memory of Mrs. Walter Paepke, who sold the land for development. The only automobiles allowed into town would be limited to a network of "delivery alleys," as shown in the very detailed plan drawn by architect/planner Fritz Benedict in 1969. All public movement would be by foot and a fleet of bicycles, maintained by the city police force.
2) Change the name "Aspen," by public referendum, to "Fat City." This would prevent greedheads, land-rapers and other human jackals from capitalizing on the name "Aspen." Thus, Snowmass-at-Aspen—recently sold to Kiaser/Aetna of Oakland, California—would become "Snowmass-at-Fat-City." The Aspen Wildcats—whose main backers include the First National City Bank of New York and the First Boston Capital Corp.—would have to be called the "Fat City Wildcats." All road signs and maps would have to be changed from ASPEN to FAT CITY. The local post office and chamber of commerce would be forced to use the new name. "Aspen," Colorado, would no longer exist—and the psychic alterations of this change would be massive in the world of commerce: Fat City Ski Fashions, the Fat City Slalom Club, Fat City Music Festival, Fat City Institute for Humanistic Studies...etc. The main advantage here is that changing the name of the town would have no major effect on the town itself, or on those people who came here because it's a good place to live. What effect the name change might have on those who came here to buy low, sell high and then move on is fairly obvious...and eminently desirable. These swine should be fucked, broken and driven across the land like the rotten maggots they are.
3) Drug sales must be controlled. My first act as sheriff will be to install, on the courthouse lawn, a bastinado platform and a set of stocks—in order to punish dishonest dope dealers in a proper public fashion. Each year these scum-suckers cheat millions of people out of millions of dollars; as a breed, they rank with subdividers and used-car salesmen...and the Sheriff's Department will gladly hear complaints against dealers at any hour of the day or night, with immunity from prosecution guaranteed to the complaining party—provided the complaint is valid. (It should be noted, on this point in the platform, that any sheriff of any county in Colorado is legally responsible for enforcing *all* state laws regarding drugs—even those few he might personally disagree with. The statutes provide for malfeasance penalties of up to $100 in each instance, in cases of willful nonenforcement.... But it should also be noted that the statutes provide for many other penalties, in many strange and unlikely circumstances, and as sheriff I shall make myself aware of *all* these, without exception. So any vengeful, ill-advised dingbat who might presume to bring malfeasance charges against my office should be quite sure of his

or her facts.) And in the meantime, it will be the general philosophy of the sheriff's office that no drug worth taking should be sold for money. Nonprofit sales will be viewed as borderline cases, and judged on their merits. But all sales for money-profit will be punished severely. This approach, we feel, will establish a unique and very human ambiance in the Aspen (or Fat City) drug culture—which is already so much a part of our local reality that only a fascist lunatic would talk about trying to "eliminate it." So the only realistic approach is to make life in this town very ugly for all profiteers—in drugs and all other fields.

4) Hunting and fishing should be forbidden to all nonresidents, with the exception of those who can obtain the signed endorsement of a resident—who will then be legally responsible for any violation or abuse committed by the nonresident he has "signed for." Fines will be heavy, and the general policy will be merciless prosecution of all offenders. But—as in the case of the proposed city name-change—this "local endorsement" plan should have no effect on anyone except greedy, dangerous kill-freaks who are a menace wherever they go. This new plan would have no effect on residents—except those who *endorse* visiting "sportsmen." By this approach—making hundreds or even thousands of *individuals* personally responsible for protecting the animals, fish and birds who live here—we would create a sort of de facto game preserve, without the harsh restrictions that will necessarily be forced on us if these bloodthirsty geeks keep swarming in here each autumn and shooting everything they see.

5) The sheriff and his deputies should *never* be armed in public. Every urban riot, shoot-out and bloodbath (involving guns) in recent memory has been set off by some trigger-happy cop in a fear frenzy. And no cop in Aspen has had to use a gun for so many years that I feel safe in offering a $2 cash reward to anybody who can recall such an incident in writing (Box K-3, Aspen). Under a normal circumstance, a pistol-grip Mace-bomb such as the MK-V made by General Ordnance is more than enough to quickly wilt any violence problem that is likely to emerge in Aspen. And anything the MK-V can't handle would require reinforcements anyway...in which case the response would be geared at all times to massive retaliation: a brutal attack with guns, bombs, pepper-foggers, wolverines, and all other weapons deemed necessary to restore the civic peace. The whole notion of disarming the police is to *lower* the level of violence—while guaranteeing, at the same time, a terrible punishment to anyone stupid enough to attempt violence on an unarmed cop.

6) It will be the policy of the sheriff's office to savagely harass those engaged in any form of land-rape. This will be done by acting, with utmost dispatch, on any and all righteous complaints. My first act in office—after setting up the machinery for punishing dope dealers—will be to establish a research bureau to provide facts on which any citizen can file a writ of seizure, a writ of stoppage, a writ of fear, of horror...yes...even a writ of assumption...against any greedhead who has managed to get around our antiquated zoning laws and set up a tar vat, scum drain or gravel pit. These writs will be pursued with overweening zeal...and always within the letter of the law.

Selah.

'reak Power' Candidate May Be the

ANTHONY RIPLEY
ecial to The New York Times

PEN, Colo., Oct. 13 — It 't really supposed to be litical campaign, at least in the ordinary sense, n Hunter S. Thompson— or, satirist, master of the on, connoisseur of the ab- —announced that he was ning for the office of nty sheriff with the support of "freak power." It was a joke, a diversionary tactic. It was a wild, raucous noise raised from e underground of this pres- gious tourist city famous r its skiing, its classical usic festivals and its Insti- ute for Humanistic Studies.

he Talk of the ampaign

But whatever it was meant o be, it is no longer that. The fact is that Hunter Thompson's bizarre campaign, probably the most bizarre on the American scene today, may well make him the next sheriff of Pitkin County.

And even if it doesn't, it will have generated enough political passion to last placid Aspen another century. For this year as always, while the national political figures grab the headlines and monopolize the television screen, it is the hot local campaign like Mr. Thompson's that arouses the most interest in any one place.

The reason Mr. Thompson has a chance of winning, as a matter of political arithmetic, is that in a three-way race his two opponents—the Democratic incumbent, Sheriff Carrol Whitmire, and the Republican challenger, Glenn M. Ricks—may split the vote and let him slip in by default.

But the reason Mr. Thompson is in any position to think about political arithmetic at all is that at a time when Aspen is deeply worried about where it is going and why, he has touched a public nerve with some fundamental questions of value and direction.

The trouble with Aspen is that it is such success. For wealthy have ski runs with of 3,300 feet with the beat bums of a d tion, and t longhairs.

Developme mushrooming the Roaring F runs along giant ski with them b ing sense among this of 2,350 per

The word ploitation" land" are bite is d Aspen Mo the only s now Butte lands, Snc and the n all outside County.

Apartm ums are the newly along t areas. Th tive buil sion arc them.

Such ditionally solid A progress of Aspe dents s turning remote somethi suburb.

For

David Hiser for The New York Times

Hunter S. Thompson next to a portrait of J. Edgar Hoover

IT WAS terrifying. I was on the verge of having to take over the whole law enforcement machinery of Pitkin County, Colorado, on my own terms, with a campaign platform that guaranteed (in a last-minute compromise with my own lawyers) that no sheriff's deputy would eat mescaline on duty.

It was weird, Bubba. Take my word for it. When I finally lost by only four percentage points, it was the happiest day of my life. I'd still be in jail if I'd won.

The system was not ready yet for Freak Power. But it was close. I decided to take a break. Hollywood. Las Vegas. Saigon.

But it didn't work that way. In the winter of 1971 I found myself in Washington, covering presidential politics full-time, and I was still angry.

The next two years were weird—but that is another story. Fuck it.

Politics is like the stock market: It's a bad business for people who can't afford to lose.

—Richard Nixon, New Hampshire, 1968

A LOT OF people have said that—but in my own memory it is always Richard Nixon in the winter of 1968 as he glanced up from his meager breakfast in the Manchester Holiday Inn, just before he and Pat Buchanan took off in a rented yellow Mercury for the local TV station. They were going to make a "Nixon for President" commercial that they had to pay for in cash before anyone would let him in front of a camera.

Nixon paid. Or maybe Patrick did. "The Boss" was not short of money in those days, or at least he never seemed to be.

He had two pin-stripe blue "senator" suits and a boxful of crisp white shirts and a few pints of gin and a fine little four-passenger, two-pilot Lear jet that he was very proud of.

Nixon gave me a tour of it one night, pointing out a few things that he especially liked about it—including the extremely high cruising speed, which was "actually a hell of a lot faster than they *tell* you it is," he said. "This thing is so goddamn fast that you don't even *need* a crapper." He laughed and pointed vaguely toward the rear of the plane, where he seemed to think a lavatory might have been, back in the good old days.... "It makes the crapper obsolete," he said. "You don't even have *time* to crap!"

Nixon was fun in those days, and so was the New Hampshire primary. It was where you could see evil *up close*. There is *no avoiding* the goddamn candidates in New Hampshire. They are usually boomers and Judas goats with nothing to lose and usually no Secret Service protection either. New Hampshire is like the good old days, as Mr. Nixon might say, when ESPN used to televise *every game* in the first round of the NCAA basketball tournament—the round where the crazies show up and every once in a while beat somebody *big*. Or almost. Like when a crippled seven-man team called the "Delta Devils" from Mississippi Valley State almost derailed top-ranked Duke in 1986 and lost only because all of their players fouled out in the final moments.

NIXON'S THE ONE!

NEW HAMPSHIRE was like that, too. It was one of those places where anybody who was *really* into politics (the true junkies) could always be found in the winter of every fourth year, when the first crowd of candidates arrived. It was like opening day of the racing season at Saratoga. The *players* always showed up.

The New Hampshire primary was so much fun and so absolutely necessary for understanding the campaign in any year that a lot of people felt an almost *genetic imperative* to be there, like the whooping cranes in Nebraska.

I was one of them for a while. I used to make reservations two years in advance—even *four*—for my clean, well-lighted room at the now-famous Wayfarers' Inn in Manchester, where the hot rods stayed and all the action was....

The mood of the Wayfarers' was like a casino. Losing in New Hampshire was usually permanent, and winning was a guaranteed fast ride to *somewhere*—maybe the White House—or at least a fiery exit. Probably soon, but so what?

It is what they call a "heady atmosphere"—like hanging around in the paddock and feeling the horses. On one night, just a few hours before the polls opened, I came back to my room and found that it had been taken over by Walter Cronkite....

I have never forgiven him for it.

But I forgave the Wayfarers'. They had no choice. It was purely a matter of *muscle*, and I didn't have enough. That's politics, Bubba. It almost never changes.

But I *did* have the winning candidate that year, and Walter didn't. (He has never forgiven me for *that*, either—even though, later, I tried to *include him*. He is a stupid, spiteful, vicious, back-stabbing old fraud of a man who is not what he seems to be, and— Whoops. Never mind that. I must have been brooding on George Bush. That swine! No. Walter was *never* like that. He is an honest man, and George Bush is a raving human sacrifice. The difference is huge.)

I HAD RESERVATIONS at the Wayfarers' in February of '92—but I cancelled, more or less at the last moment, and decided to stay away and miss my chance of locking on to a front-runner....

I was smart, I thought. Fuck those people. George Bush was unbeatable, and these Democrats were a gang of second-string bums who were probably looking for a jump on 1996.... You bet! Just spell my name right. I am running for president and you're not—so get out of my goddamn way, if you don't vote, and the next time you see me coming, Bubba, you better *run*.

CHAPTER 3
SUMMER OF '91

Nightmare in Woody Creek...Invasion of the power-mongers...Armed standoff with George Bush, trapped in a dead-end valley with the prime minister of England...Airport seized by suicidal gunman, Secret Service paralyzed...Just how weird can you stand it, Bubba, before your love will crack?...

The summer is over, the harvest is in, and we are not saved.

— Jeremiah, 8:20

JULY AND AUGUST are lightning months in the Rockies. Sometimes you get thunder, but not always. On some nights it's only lightning, with no rain at all, and no thunder...ungodly lightning storms, wild blasts and flashes every 10 or 15 seconds for two straight hours. They call it "summer lightning," and a lot of people get whacked by it—like what happened to Lee Trevino a few years back when he was wandering around in a thunderstorm with his one-iron over his shoulder. *Whack!* Right beside him. Black hole in the green, 66 billion volts, but he lived and later said, "Not even God can hit a one-iron."

ON SOME DAYS you wonder what it all means. And on some days you find out. It's like suddenly seeing a huge black pig in your headlights when you're running 80 miles an hour on ice. *Boom.* Total clarity. No more gray area.

Some people live for these moments, these terrible flashes of clarity and naked truth, and on some days I am one of them.... But not always. It is not a lot different from the rush that comes from electroshock therapy, or getting hit by lightning. *Zang!* Immediate fire in the nuts, bulging eyes and the smell of burning hair.

It is an acquired taste. The first one's free, but after that you have to really like it.

When I was 15 years old I used to run around naked on the Cherokee Park golf course in Louisville on summer nights when the thunder and lightning happened and the greens were drenched with rain. One night I was huddled under a big elm tree about halfway down the long first hole, which rolled gently up to a hill above the lake, when I was suddenly blasted about 10 feet up in the air by a jolt so terrible that I couldn't even feel it until I was tumbling and twitching on the downhill side of No. 3, and when I looked back to where I had been, I saw the tree was on fire and split down the middle. It was hissing and popping and sputtering in the rain, and when I finally went back for my clothes, they were burned and scorched and the gooseneck putter that I'd had in my hand was burned black and twisted like a pretzel.

That is lightning, Bubba. Ben Franklin got off easy. And they say he wasn't naked, but you never know.... Ben was weird, but he had enough sense to get a patent on it, even with one of his arms charred halfway off.

He was alone when it happened, knocked unconscious for eight or nine minutes.... Then he crawled back into his workshop and made a new arm for himself, which he attached to his bicep with magnets. (That's why you always see Ben Franklin in long, puffy sleeves, and why he always carried a cane.)

Some people hated Ben Franklin, but it never seemed to

bother him. He was extremely smart, and he had a keen understanding of politics. . . . He was dirty and filthy and covered with fleas, and he took his women by the twos and by threes.

Whoops. Scratch that one. Just kidding. Ben kept himself clean as a whistle—except when it rained, and then he went all to pieces.

HISTORY IS FULL of these oddities. Some things happen for no good reason. And then other things happen and suddenly you have a chain of craziness on your hands, and sometimes it can't be controlled. The craziness swarms all over you. It happened to me one afternoon in July about two years ago. Maybe three. It's a matter of public record.

I was pushed and leaned on like the Marquis de Sade. In the summer of 1990 I came under serious attack by the forces of evil. I was in full retreat, like Lee after Gettysburg, and my spirit was feeling weak—and it was then, at my weakest, that I was backed into a corner and attacked on my own turf by the president of the United States, the prime minister of England, the Secret Service, the press, the liberals, John Denver, the police, Pat Buchanan, all my creditors, many foreigners and a coalition of extremely rich Nazis who had swarmed into Aspen that summer to mingle and wallow in the glitz.

They were ugly people, but they were very expensively dressed and they had a certain glow about them that said they were in charge. Which was true. They were the rich and the powerful, the elite suave friends of the New World Order.

And I was definitely not one of them. I was on the run, a crude outlaw about to be captured and put in some kind of cage for the amusement of George and Maggie.

It was weird, Bubba—and then it began to get weirder. Take my word for it. I was there.

THE SHERIFF CALLED me at noon and said he felt trouble coming. "I feel like I'm going crazy," he said. "There's a killer on the loose and he's holed up in Woody Creek. And Bush will be here tomorrow."

"Don't worry," I said. "We'll bomb the bastard. Where is he?"

"Whitehorse Springs," he said. "We have him surrounded, but we can't get near the house. He says he'll kill anybody who comes close."

"Well," I said, "don't go close. He can't escape. Whitehorse Springs is a death trap. There's no way out."

"That's not the problem," he said. "Of course we can wait him out—but the Secret Service wants to kill him right now. He's up on the mountain in a bunker with hundreds of weapons, and he's looking right down on the airport."

"So what?" I said. "Get a helicopter and put a gas bomb down on him. That will flush him out, then you can nail him when he flees."

"Nail him?" said the sheriff. "What do you mean, 'nail' him? Are you nuts? I can't just murder the poor bastard. It would be horrible publicity for the town—and besides, he hasn't done anything."

"What?" I said. "I thought you said he was a killer. Who did he kill?"

"Nobody," said the sheriff. "He's harmless."

I felt tricked. *"Then why the fuck are you telling me the Secret Service wants to kill him?"* I screamed.

"Because they *think* he's going to kill the president," he hissed. "That's why! He has a bazooka up there! He has rocket launchers! He's *crazy*! And he hates George Bush!"

"So do I," I said. "Do they want to kill me, too?"

"Not yet," he said. "But things could change, if—"

"Okay," I said quietly. The president of the United States was flying into the Aspen airport tomorrow—and so was Margaret Thatcher, the prime minister of England. They were coming to Woody Creek for a summit conference.

"Ye fucking gods," I muttered.

"Yeah," he said. "The fat is in the fire."

The sheriff hung up. I decided to follow the developments on CNN, when a car roared into my driveway, and then I heard doors slamming and my friend Loren Jenkins rushed in, jabbering wildly about roadblocks and killers and cops gone crazy with fear and how they were on their way—

"What?" I shouted. "Cops?" I leaped up and grasped wildly on the counter for the remote that would slam-lock the front gates, but it was gone.... No, I thought. This can't be true! Not again! Impossible! They won't attack me. They wouldn't dare!

Loren ignored me and grabbed the telephone, stabbing frantically down on the keyboard. "Oh god!" he screamed. "What the fuck is my number?"

"What number?" I said. "You bastard! Where is my fucking remote? My gate! Close the gate! Fuck this! I can't stand it anymore! Why cops?"

"They're crazy!" he snapped. "They're trying to kill my wife!"

I found the remote in a pile with seven others and heard a distant clang of steel bars down by the road as the electric gates slammed shut and the 220-volt transformer kicked in. Then I rushed around the house to secure the doors and windows and dark shades.... Just as I hit the slam button for the garage door, I heard somebody screaming and saw a figure sprinting up the driveway toward the house with a machine gun in his hands.

Holy shit, I thought. It's true! Here they come! I leaped back into the porch and reached for the shotgun on the rack, but it was gone.... I had put all the guns in the vault because I was expecting a visit from the Secret Service and I didn't want to alarm them with a display of high-powered weapons. Not with the president coming into the valley....

Suddenly a man's body came slithering under the garage door, just before it slammed shut, and I recognized my friend Cromwell just in time to keep from bashing him with a shovel.

"You Nazi bastard!" he screamed. "You tried to electrocute me!" He had taken a great shock when he tried to open the gate and another when he climbed over it. He rushed up the stairs and yelled frantically at me, "They're coming! Get ready! Hide everything! They're killing people at the tavern."

"What?" I shouted. "Cops?"

"Hundreds of them!" he moaned. "They're all over the road with shotguns and rifles. They want you!"

WELL, I THOUGHT. Why not? Those crazy shit-eating dogs! I was innocent and they knew it—but they were coming to kill me anyway. Probably with firebombs, like they did to those poor screwheads who grabbed Patty Hearst. Right. Seal off the house and set us on fire with phosphorous grenades—even if we tried to surrender. Fuck them, I thought. They are pigs! Coming to kill me because they couldn't do it in court. Shit on them. Get the guns, call the lawyers, turn on the screechers, put voltage everywhere. Burn them. Injure them. Extract a terrible price. Like the Alamo. We will fight to the death.

It made perfect sense at the time. It was the time of George Bush, the 10th triumphant year of the relentless greed, looting and punishment that was the "Reagan Revolution." It was a heady time, and Woody Creek had become the center of it.

LOREN WAS STILL screeching into the telephone in the kitchen. "Oh god!" he wailed. "She won't answer! I can't get through to her. She's trapped behind roadblocks!"

I grabbed the other phone and called the sheriff, who answered instantly and called me a fool for tying up his hot line when a crisis was happening. "It's a nightmare," he said. "I'm surrounded by crazies! They want to attack."

"Why!" I screamed. "What have I done? I'm innocent!"

"So what?" he said. "So am I. But it's out of our hands now. The goddamn Secret Service thinks we have a suicidal assassin on our hands, and the goddamn Brits are afraid he is an IRA hit man! They'll kill all of us if they think we're a danger to the prime minister. And some of them suspect the hit man is you."

"Ye gods," I said.

LIKE MOST "desperate stand-off" stories, this one petered out harmlessly when the Crazed Gunman ran out of amphetamine extract and agreed to surrender in exchange for two cans of food for his cat. On his way to the state mental facility, he confessed that he hadn't even known Bush and Thatcher were coming to town, and he had no idea why police with rifles had surrounded his house. He thought it was a plot by his wife and her psychiatrist to get him out of the way.

"Why not?" said the sheriff. "It happens all the time."

He was kidding, of course. Only a madman would believe that a lustful shrink might seize control of his wife's mind, just because it was *there*. Not in this day and age. They have rules.

SURE THEY DO—just like in politics, where the only *real* rule is *Don't Get Caught*. And even that one is constantly being tested, these days. (Look at Oliver North, the charming gap-toothed ex–U.S. Marine officer. He somehow beat seventeen felony charges, including treason, and used it as a springboard to martyrdom, riches and the Republican U. S. Senate nomination from Virginia two years later.)

I brood on these things. It is one of those old habits, like date-rape, and cigarettes, which I like too much to quit.

PROBABLY IT WAS the humiliation of having George Bush create panic on my own turf that drove the stake through my gizzard. There were a hell of a lot of upscale, maximum-security destination resorts in the world where he could have scheduled a week long assignation with the randy British PM (Camp David, Hong Kong, Bermuda, Alcatraz, Paris, the Isle of Man), all of them safer, more neutral and more electronically prepared than a politically disturbed little valley in Colorado where random violence and awkward behavior are an accepted way of life, and bodies are found on the cliffs below the road every spring.

But Bush went ahead and tightened the screws on me anyway, by declaring war on Iraq about three days after he got here. He and Maggie were forced to cut their tryst short and stand together on the lawn of then–U.S. Ambassador to the Court of St. James, Henry Cato, who lives just over the hill from the Big Boom Experimental Free-fire Range at the Woody Creek Rod and Gun Club, where the earth is sometimes split by sharp, high-impact explosions that light up the valley at night. It was a decidedly odd place for the first New World Order summit meeting, and public opinion compelled me to take it personally.

There is no such thing as paranoia.
—F. X. Leach, Altamont, 1969

Meanwhile, back at the White House, the well-disciplined "Four More Years" machine was bloated with hubris and running at top speed. The wizards in charge of making the White House winter book on Campaign '92 were so arrogant and blindly overconfident about reelecting the sleazy Bush/Quayle team that, early in 1991, the Director of Presidential Personnel sent the following Confidential Memo to all the campaign junkies and key staffers from the 1988 election, advising that their services would not be required in 1992. It sent nasty shock waves through the ranks of the proven Pros who thought they were about to go to war again, for the usual big money and easy venues—and then found themselves useless and essentially out of work until 1996. Many felt crippled and betrayed, and I was one of them.

WELCOME TO THE UNSPEAKABLE, WELCOME TO THE TANK

THE WHITE HOUSE

WASHINGTON

February 26, 1991

TO: All Political Appointees

FROM: Director of Presidential Personnel

RE: 1992 Campaign

A great many of you have been contacting my office, the Chief of Staff's office, and the RNC about returning to the positions you held during the 1988 national campaign. We are heartened that so many of you have expressed willingness to give up your agency jobs for the hectic pace and low pay of campaign spots.

With few exceptions, however, neither the White House nor the RNC will be adding campaign staff until two months before the Convention; even then, we expect to be putting on only a very few pollsters, opposition researchers, speechwriters, and floor organizers. The reason for this shift is just what you probably expect: at this point, there is no reason to believe we need to run a national campaign in 1992 in order to keep hold of the Executive. Our Commander in Chief has seen to that!

We will, however, be encouraging each of you to sign on with one or more of the Congressional campaigns the GOP has a chance of winning. Jim Buckley at the NRSC and Ed Rollins at the NRCC are currently putting together grass-roots teams and strategy pods for every State and District, and we encourage you to contact them to become part of the team in each of your respective home States or Districts. Given our success at holding the White House, there is no reason to be discouraged about our ability to take control of the Senate -- and the House.

Each of you played a crucial role in 1988, and we hope each of you will continue to work for the GOP both in your agencies and in the 1992 Congressional campaigns.

Chase Untermeyer

BUSH UBER ALLES:

From wimp to warrior and back to wimp again... How I shrewdly joined the GOP conspiracy to dump George Bush in '92...

IN THE WINTER OF '91, George Bush was a lock for reelection. His "approval rating" had rocketed from 41 percent in August to 89 percent six months later. The smart money said he was unbeatable in 1992. One by one the big-name Democratic front-runners decided, in public, that '92 was not looking like a real good year for taking on an incumbent GOP president who was loved by 9 out of every 10 people on any street corner in America. His bogus "War in the Gulf" had made him a hero all over the world, and children wanted to kiss him.

George Bush was in charge that year. He walked tall and kicked ass. George and his generals were the toast of the civilized world, and later that year they became almost godlike, as "democracy" swept the world and the Soviet Union crumbled.... It was a heady time, folks; the USA was definitely Number One, and so was George Bush. He was The Man.

Records of the time (see preceding Untermeyer memo) show that Bush and his people were so utterly confident of getting reelected in '92 that they formally disbanded their national campaign staff. "We are like tits on a boar hog," said a suddenly unemployed speechwriter. "They sent me a one-way ticket to Utah, where I got assigned to some yoyo running for governor on the straight Nazi ticket. Shit, we had to flee the state on election night, and I haven't worked since."

NEITHER HAS George Bush. No president in American history has fallen so far, so fast, as Bush did between the summer of '91 and the summer of '92....

He dipped about 55 percentage points in those 12 baffling months, and in the end he was just another oil lobbyist from Texas.

The main problem George Bush had in the summer of '91 is that nobody in big-time Republican politics really owed him anything. He was the president, but so what? Richard Nixon had also been the president, and look what happened to him. When Nixon became an embarrassment to the GOP, they dropped him like a stone and hunkered down, all but conceding the 1976 presidential race to a lightweight, nonthreatening peanut farmer from Georgia named Jimmy Carter.

There was no hope for any Republican candidate in '76, they felt; it was better to "let the wounds heal," they said, and turn the terrible responsibilities of the White House over to a maverick, small-state Southern governor with no real power base and no hope of reelection.

It was a strategic retreat for the GOP. Let the Democrats reap the whirlwind of the public rage and loss of faith in government that came in the wake of Watergate. The guaranteed nightmare job of taking over the federal government, after Nixon, with a gang of local pols from Georgia would almost certainly paralyze Carter and turn him to jelly by 1980, when they would have a brand-new contender. Until then, Carter was merely a caretaker, a short-term lessee.

The strategy worked like a charm, and in 1980 Jimmy Carter was swept away like offal by the "Reagan Revolution," which ushered in eight years of berserk looting of the federal treasury and the economic crippling of the middle class.

That was the eighties, folks. That was the feeding frenzy of the New Rich, who found themselves wallowing in excess profits as their maximum income tax rate got chopped down to 31 percent and who were welcomed like brothers in the White House at all hours of the day or night.

GEORGE BUSH barely had enough clout to keep his own son out of prison. When silly young Neil got caught in the web of the Savings & Loan scandal, George instantly cut him loose and said he had total confidence in the federal court system, which would surely vindicate Neil—provided that he was telling the truth.

Which was wishful thinking, as fate would have it. Neil had peddled more (alleged) influence and accepted more flagrant favors than the whore of Babylon during his brief stint as a sort of executive greeter for Silverado Savings & Loan in Denver, and he was not of a mood to repay any of the huge tips and free loans he'd received as kickbacks in exchange for the massive unsecured *big* loans he doled out to his new friends in the Colorado money business.

He walked anyway—but it wasn't easy. In the end he was allowed to slip through the cracks. He avoided prison, but his father paid a heavy price for it in public esteem and in the eyes of GOP power-mongers and long-term strategists, who viewed him as a wimp and a stooge.

IT WAS about that time that I too abandoned big-time politics as a natural way of life. I rejected many lush offers to cover the upcoming presidential campaign, and "went to ground," as they say, like a common beast of the forest. I did, after all, have a million-dollar contract to write my long-awaited sex novel—and the last thing I needed that winter was another low-rent, no-win nightmare on another campaign trail.

Fuck those people. Anger and lust are the main fuels of a serious presidential campaign, and anybody who signs on for the long haul *will* be a jabbering wreck on Election Day.

I wanted no part of it. Bush would win easily, I thought, and all the Democratic candidates looked lame. It was a bad year for anger and lust.

REPUBLICAN PRESIDENTIAL TASK FORCE

This is to certify that at the behest of President George Herbert Walker Bush an American Flag was dedicated in the Rotunda of the United States Capitol for:

MR. HUNTER THOMPSON

In recognition of a commitment to defending our agenda of peace, prosperity and continued economic growth through the election of a Republican Majority to the United States Senate in 1990.

Ronald Reagan
Founder

George Bush
President

THE FIRST thing I did after locking the gates 24 hours a day was to join the Republican Presidential Task Force—just to keep an eye on things, I told myself. If I'm not playing, these buggers must be watched.

The membership fee was $120, and a lot of people laughed at me—but not for long: When my benefits started pouring in, even bedrock Democrats were impressed. My social status went up about nine points a week and my enemies no longer sneered when I walked into the post office. They were baffled and put off-balance as my lockbox filled up with gifts, flags, photos, medals and special-delivery letters from the White House. On one day in June, I received a full-size American flag, signed by Ronald Reagan, an autographed photo of George Bush, two gold-plated presidential tie tacks, a full-size faux-bronze *Medal of Freedom* replica, a huge pyrite-slab coin with a bust of Richard Nixon on it, and a stunning engraved hologram Presidential Task Force laser graphite "credit card" that looked so official that I often used it to guarantee personal checks at fine restaurants all over the country.

Nobody ever challenged or even doubted my strange new credibility. Because it was *real*. My bona fides were genuine and so were my full-access Congressional hot-line phone numbers that I could call 24 hours a day for issues-briefings on any bill or national problem.... It was amazing. In less than two years' time I had gone from personal enemy of the president to a position of high trust and confidential access to the highest levels of policy and power in Washington. And if that was "sleeping with the enemy," as a few of my mentally challenged friends said, well... it was blue-chip political journalism.

In fact I am still a member of the goddamn thing. It was not a bad card to have in my wallet when I was falsely arrested on sex, bombs and drugs charges. My people stood behind me. They never wavered. And, in the end, I made them proud. It was a harsh lesson to all those who would fuck with the innocent.

Editor's note: *For a further explanation of our unprecedented Campaign Time Line,* *please refer to page xvii.*

TIME LINE, CAMPAIGN '92

Mon	**05 Mar 90**	Lee Atwater collapses
Thu	**02 Aug 90**	Iraq invades Kuwait
Mon	**06 Aug 90**	Operation "Desert Shield" activated
Thu	**09 Aug 90**	UN declares annexation of Kuwait "null and void"
Wed	**03 Oct 90**	East and West Germany unite as Federal Republic of Germany
Thu	**29 Nov 90**	UN Security Council authorizes force against Iraq
Wed	**16 Jan 91**	Activating Operation "Desert Storm," allied forces initiate an air strike against Iraq
Sat	**23 Feb 91**	U.S.-led ground forces enter Gulf War
Wed	**27 Feb 91**	Kuwait liberated
Fri	**29 Mar 91**	**Republican National Chairman Lee Atwater, who had been hospitalized on and off for the past year with a brain tumor, dies. Dark day for GOP.**

Thu	11 Apr 91	Gulf War ends
Tue	30 Apr 91	Paul Tsongas announces for president
Wed	12 Jun 91	Boris Yeltsin elected
Sat	24 Aug 91	Mikhail Gorbachev resigns from the Communist party
Fri	13 Sep 91	Doug Wilder announces for president
Sun	15 Sep 91	Tom Harkin announces for president
Mon	30 Sep 91	Bob Kerrey announces for president
Thu	03 Oct 91	**Bill Clinton announces for president**
Sat	05 Oct 91	Eugene McCarthy announces for president
Sun	06 Oct 91	**Sexual harassment charges reported against Supreme Court nominee** **Clarence Thomas, already "confirmed" by 52–48 Senate vote, is stunned by new sexual harassment charges brought by longtime aide Professor Anita Hill of the Oklahoma Law School, who finally decides she will testify against him, under oath, on nationwide TV**

McCARTHY

THE CLARENCE THOMAS HEARINGS

I FELL OFF the apolitical wagon during the Clarence Thomas hearings. After Anita Hill and her supporters finished, there were two days off. Two days to get the pro-Thomas votes to waver; I really thought Thomas could be beaten.

But I noticed that CNN's midnight raps on the hearings were taking an ugly drift: "...Well, Thomas has probably made it." And if CNN did that for two days, you bet Thomas would have it made. In a rage I sent off a long, crazy fax to the network's Ed Turner, trying to prevent them from conceding before the vote was in.

I was trying to control my environment. Since I didn't have a column, I couldn't hit hard on anything except if I got hold of the boss of all news at CNN and convinced him to alter their coverage.

I was trying to manage the news the only way I knew how. But it didn't work.

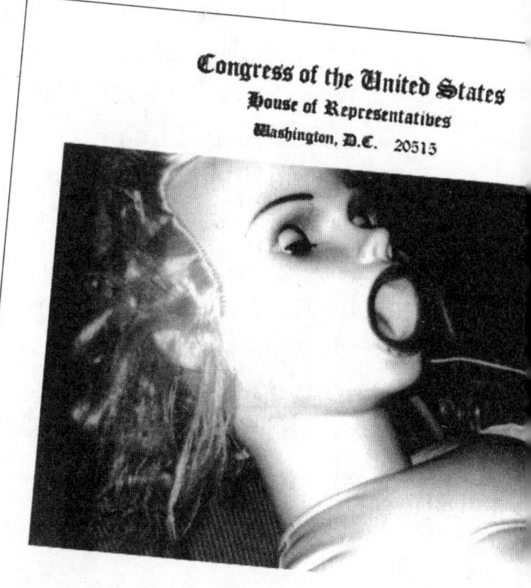
Congress of the United States
House of Representatives
Washington, D.C. 20515

15 Oct. '91
Owl Farm

ED TURNER
CNN NEWS

Dear ED:

Tue	**15 Oct 91**	**Clarence Thomas confirmed by Senate**
Mon	**21 Oct 91**	Jerry Brown announces for president
Sat	**02 Nov 91**	Jesse Jackson says he won't run for president Advising his supporters to remain neutral "free agents," Jackson announces he will not seek the presidency in 1992
Tue	**05 Nov 91**	**Upset in Pennsylvania election—Thornburgh loses**

THE SINKING OF THORNBURGH:

Early warning alarm for the GOP… Camelot goes on trial for rape…

THERE IS more and more predatory bullshit in the air these days. Yesterday I got a call from somebody who said I owed money to Harris Wofford, my old friend from the Peace Corps; we were in Sierra Leone together.

He had come out of nowhere like a heat-seeking missile and destroyed U.S. Attorney General Dick Thornburgh in Pennsylvania. Wonderful. Harris is a senator now, and the White House creature is not. He blew a 44-point lead in three weeks, like Humpty-Dumpty.... Whoops! Off the wall like a big lizard egg. The White House had seen no need for a safety net.

It was a major disaster for the Bush brain trust and every GOP political pro in America, from the White House all the way down to City Hall in places like Denver and Tupelo. The whole Republican party was left stunned and shuddering like a hound dog passing a peach pit. (At least that's what they said in Tupelo, where a local GOP man flipped out and ran off to Biloxi with a fat young boy from one of the rich local families.... Then he tried to blame it on Harris Wofford when they arrested him. He was ruined. Bail was only $5,000, but none of his friends would sign for it. Most were mainly professional Republicans and bankers who had once been in the Savings & Loan business, along with Neil Bush.)

Tue	**03 Dec 91**	Last U.S. hostage released from Lebanon
Tue	**03 Dec 91**	White House Chief of Staff John Sununu resigned today after being the center of ethical and professional controversy for many months

ANYWAY, Thornburgh is now seeking night work in the bank business somewhere on the outskirts of Pittsburgh. It is an ugly story. He decided to go out on his own—like Lucifer, who plunged into hell—and he got beaten like a redheaded stepchild. He was mangled and humiliated. It was the worst Republican public disaster since Watergate.

The GOP was plunged into national fear. How could it happen? Dick Thornburgh had sat on the right hand of God. As A.G., he had stepped out like some arrogant knight from the Round Table and declared that his Boys—15,000 or so Justice Department prosecutors—were no longer subject to the rules of the federal court system. The White House lost more than a Senate seat when Thornburgh went down: It was a major signal that Bush and his braintrust could be beaten. It also raised health care and the economy to the forefront of Clinton's campaign agenda.

But Wofford's win went largely unnoticed in the national frenzy over the "Kennedy rape trial" in Palm Beach.

Camelot was on court TV, limping into re-hab clinics and forced to deny low-rent rape accusations in the same sweaty West Palm Beach courthouse where Roxanne Pulitzer went on trial for fucking a trumpet, and lost.

It has been a long way down—not just for the Kennedys and the Democrats, but for all of us. Even the rich and the powerful are coming to understand that change can be quick in the nineties and that one of these days it will be them in the dock on TV, fighting desperately to stay out of prison.

Wed	**04 Dec 91**	Pan Am closes operations—third airline in 1991 to do so
Wed	**04 Dec 91**	David Duke announces for president
Sat	**07 Dec 91**	Fiftieth anniversary of Pearl Harbor
Sun	**08 Dec 91**	Leaders of Russia, Ukraine and Belarus announce dissolution of the Soviet Union
Tue	**10 Dec 91**	Pat Buchanan announces for president
Wed	**11 Dec 91**	**William Kennedy Smith found not guilty of rape**

Soon come. Take my word for it. I have been there, and it gives me an eerie feeling.... Indeed. There are many cells in the mansion, and more are being added every day. We are becoming a nation of jailers.

Sun	**15 Dec 91**	Florida Democrats cast the following "straw votes" for presidential candidates at the state party convention: Clinton 54%, Harkin 31%, Kerrey 10%, Tsongas 2%, Cuomo 1%, Brown 1%
Fri	**20 Dec 91**	Mario Cuomo announces he will not run
Wed	**25 Dec 91**	Gorbachev resigns as Soviet president
Wed	**25 Dec 91**	U.S. recognizes independence of 12 former Soviet republics

CHAPTER 4

1992: THE HORROR, THE HORROR

Welcome to the year of the lizard...
88 percent in the public-approval polls:
Stand back! I am the president and you're not...
The rise of the Man from Hope...

I will do what I have to do to be reelected.

—George Bush, January 3, 1992

WARREN ZEVON has a song called "Up on Re-hab Mountain." It is a gloomy tune with undertones of fear, failure and disgrace. Which pretty well describes my political attitude as 1991 finally ended.

Politics looked like a smart business to quit that year, and a lot of smart people were quitting. Or just laying low for a while, they said. Get back to the law firm and make some money, fatten up for the real campaign in 1996, when the big boys would come to bat.

George Bush was riding high. Yellow ribbons and ticker-tape parades for sick war heroes. The U.S. was Number One again, and George was eating high on the hog. He had won the Gulf War and the Cold War like Sherman marching through

Georgia. He had slipped the noose on Iran-contra and rammed a dumbo named Clarence onto the Supreme Court of the United States. Even his sons were rich, and his victorious generals were getting huge book contracts. He was the Man of the Hour. He had taken care of business. The "Reagan Revolution" had lasted for 11 years, and the top-bracket income tax rate had dropped from 88 percent to 31 percent. Many rich people called George Bush their friend. He was very well liked. Nineteen ninety-one was a good year for the Bush family. The Man could do no wrong.

It was a nasty year for anybody who wasn't a member of the Republican Presidential Task Force. The train left the station early that year, and a lot of people missed it.... George Bush was clearly a shoo-in for Four More Years. The Democrats collapsed and went limp, after they lost the War on Iraq vote in the Senate. The erstwhile Demo front-runners quietly folded their tents for '92—including Georgia senator Sam Nunn, who had his tent folded for him after he cast a courageous and principled vote against the bogus war and suffered massive ridicule for it, derailing his carefully prepared '92 presidential campaign.

Mon	**06 Jan**	**92**	FDA halts sale, use of breast implants
Tue	**07 Jan**	**92**	UN observers killed in Yugoslavia
Wed	**08 Jan**	**92**	Bush collapses in Tokyo During a state dinner at the residence of the Japanese prime minister, President Bush vomits and collapses from an intestinal virus. The visit to Japan is part of an Australian/Asian tour to promote trade concessions.
Fri	**10 Jan**	**92**	U.S. unemployment hits five-year high The jobless rate rises to 7.1 percent, an increase of 0.02 percent at the end of 1991

No governors were polled on the war question. Or at least no governors voted on it—but the five-term governor of Arkansas, a second-string 300-to-1 long shot named Bill Clinton, made sure the whole world understood that he damn well *would have* voted *for* the war, if they'd let him. He called a press conference in Little Rock and swore he was not a coward, like Sam Nunn seemed to be....

WHACK. So long, Sam. And people still wonder why Bill

Clinton lost Georgia in '92 or why Les Aspin got fired and sent away to China.... Well, wonder no more, Bubba. It was Sam Nunn. Remember that name. It will hound Bill Clinton to his grave.

The first law of controlling your environment is to get the hell off the defensive as fast as you can. Take the offensive. Attack—and be Innocent, of course.

I did not like Bill Clinton until the Gennifer Flowers story came out—his adversity got me interested.

The day he was accused, I got a phone call from Missy, my friend from the Clinton campaign, saying, Ye gods, have you seen this? How are we going to handle it? A wave of sorrow and fear and despair rolled through Clinton's campaign. They hadn't been hit with anything like that before; they were really young kids. The ones who *had* been hit with it, like Eli Segal—or James Carville—remembered Gary Hart. Whacko! Down the tubes in three days.

Wed	**15 Jan**	**92**	Yugoslav Federation dissolved
Fri	**17 Jan**	**92**	**Clinton accused of marital infidelity** **Presidential candidate Bill Clinton denies allegations of extramarital affairs, calling tabloid reports "an absolute, total lie"**
Sun	**19 Jan**	**92**	*Boston Globe* poll shows Clinton ahead in New Hampshire:

Clinton	29%
Tsongas	17%
Kerrey	16%
Brown	7%
Harkin	3%

I sent "Bill Clinton Fights Back" to the Clinton headquarters. Clinton was being overloaded with charges. What advice could I give him except to deny it? Don't get like Hart. That is how dark it became.

Thu 23 Jan 92	Arkansas government employee Gennifer Flowers alleges a long-running affair with presidential candidate Bill Clinton. Flowers also claims she has tapes of phone conversations between the two.
Sun 26 Jan 92	Bill and Hillary Clinton appear on *60 Minutes*. Although acknowledging having caused "pain in my marriage," Clinton denies charges of marital infidelity made by Gennifer Flowers.
Mon 27 Jan 92	Macy's files for bankruptcy
Mon 27 Jan 92	Making portions of taped conversations public, Flowers repeats allegation of affair with Clinton
Tue 28 Jan 92	A New Hampshire poll shows Clinton support rising from 24 percent to 30 percent
Tue 04 Feb 92	CNN poll shows Bush approval rating falling: Bush job rating: Approve 47% Disapprove 48%
Wed 05 Feb 92	Bush offers health-care plan The president proposes a $100 billion program for quality, affordable health care using tax incentives and changes in law
Thu 06 Feb 92	The *Wall Street Journal* publishes an article raising questions that Bill Clinton may have improperly avoided the draft. A former draft-board official and ROTC recruiter claims that Clinton manipulated the draft process. Clinton denies improperly avoiding the draft in 1968–69 but admits that he opposed the Vietnam War.

To Missy

1/23/92

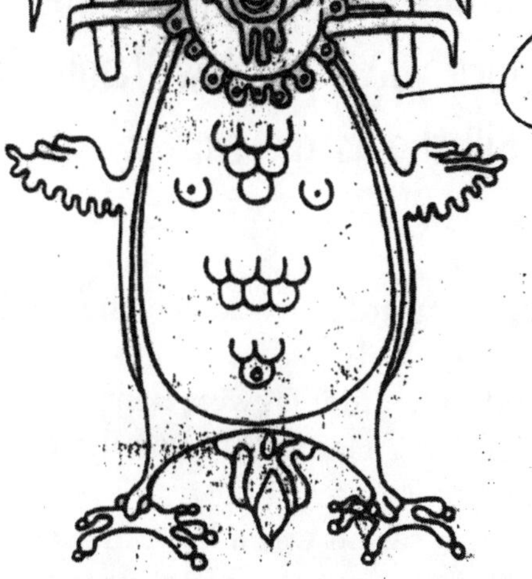

Fuck you I'm sick

The Candidate will see you Now

Bill Clinton Fights Back

Angry Sex Fiend Denies All Charges, Swears "I am NOT a Degenerate"

NEVERMORE

"I AM NOT A SLUT"

Bush collapses... Clinton flogged... The enemy of my enemy is my friend... Fuck the draft, fuck you, fuck New Hampshire... Mr. Bill shoots the gap...

THE CLINTON camp took my advice and denied everything. Which worked nicely.

The net result of the Gennifer Flowers flap was a nine-point gain for Clinton in the New Hampshire popularity polls. The pro-adultery vote had spoken.

The draft-dodger accusation was a little bit harder to beat, and it cost him about the same number of points in the polls that he'd gained on the sex charges.

I was impressed. Clinton's strategists had decided to confront these things and get them out of the way as early as possible. It was good thinking, but there was angst in his Little Rock headquarters about the possibility that Gennifer Flowers might be just the tip of the iceberg. The Man from Hope was clearly a sex addict of some kind—and although his denials might work for a while, his staff knew they had a serious adulterer on their hands, and he was not about to go into re-hab.

So what? I thought. If we start electing presidents on the basis of their sexual purity, some *real* monsters will get into the White House. I was far more concened with the way he handled the draft-dodger issue. If he'd taken a stand against the war in Vietnam, I was for him.

Bill Clinton
FOR PRESIDENT COMMITTEE

2/13

2/13/93

yes

Did you watch Nightline last night? I've received only positive phone calls this morning. My favorite: "I'm a 100% disabled Vietnam vet. And, I've decided to cast my vote for Bill Clinton. He made a choice, and I made a choice, and I sort of wish I had made his." ...

SIGNED,
A FRIEND

AF

yr. boy was good last nite. If I were in N.H. today, I'd go out + hustle votes for him. Fuck Koppel. He's been on the White House payroll for years.
Let me know if I can help. OK

HST

Mon	**10 Feb 92**	Ex-champ Mike Tyson convicted of rape
Tue	**11 Feb 92**	Cuomo New Hampshire write-in drive announced
Wed	**12 Feb 92**	Bush formally announces his candidacy for reelection
Wed	**12 Feb 92**	**Bill Clinton discloses the text of a December 3, 1969, letter written while a student at Oxford University to army Colonel Eugene Holmes thanking him for "saving me from the draft" by ROTC assignment**
Sat	**15 Feb 92**	A Milwaukee jury finds Jeffrey L. Dahmer sane and guilty of 15 killings involving torture and sex

FURTHER ADVENTURES WITH THE MOJO WIRE

There is some shit I won't eat—unless they pay me to eat it on TV in prime time.

—Walt Disney

PEOPLE THINK I watch TV too much, but they are wrong. There is a huge difference between merely "watching" TV and learning to respond aggressively to it. The difference, for most people, is the difference between the living and dying of their own brains.

The lesson is simple, yet it must be learned: If all you get from watching TV most of your life is the jumble of disconnected information it imparts, you are doomed to a life of fear and confusion—especially if you receive 500 or 600 channels 24 hours a day, like I do. The difference between Dan Rather on CBS and a Crazy Wilbur pimping junk jewelry on the RIP-U home shopping network is not easy to see or grasp when you've been watching the whole world happening constantly on three 40-inch Interactive HD/black matrix Mitsubishi TV monitors that make Bill Clinton's head appear twice the size of yours, and his voice so pure and real that it sounds like it's coming from the depth of your own throat, all day and all night for 55 straight months.

This is what happens when circumstances force you to acquire too much professional equipment all at once—which is always a dangerous thing, and many good people have been taken within the system because of it.

(Indeed. "Within the system." That is police speak for "jail." Behind bars. Locked up.... As in: "He was apprehended for being guilty and taken into the apparatus of the federal prison system." So long, Bubba. No more fun for you. Ever.)

Whoops, wandering again, but not much—because any talk of punishment always leads back to thoughts of Bill Clinton. President Clinton, from Arkansas. He has a visceral hatred of people who break the law....Indeed, but we will get to that later. We should keep it in mind for now, because it has a lot to do with my generally awkward personal relationship with the man we call "Mr. Bill."

It began, somehow, with a simple impulse to feed something into the maw of a Canon 881-X Laser Color World-Scan fax machine that had come into my possession more or less by accident. But I quickly took to it, as they say, and soon I was able to communicate instantly, on paper, with almost everybody in the world who could read English or even have it translated for them.

There is nothing new about the technology of sending printed pages across a telephone wire. I had been doing it for 20 years with a Xerox machine that we called the "Mojo Wire," which was basically a portable Telex unit that was utterly useless unless the person on the other end of the telephone line also had a Mojo machine and understood how to operate it under conditions of severe personal stress.

The Mojo was so expensive to buy and so maddeningly complex to use that nobody except the Bank of America, *Rolling Stone,* and the *New York Times* could afford the luxury of having one on the premises, and it was out of the question to risk putting a portable Mojo in the hands of some wandering journalist who might be a drinker.

The game changed, however, when suddenly everybody had a simpler one, and they called it the fax. Even Charles Manson got one, and Gary Hart was selling them on credit in Moscow. You could buy one in Denver for $600. Or $60, if you were willing to ignore that it might be a stolen unit that would always print the original owner's name on the top of every page.

Ho, ho. The fax culture is very flexible, offering many

opportunities for random abuse and hooliganism. Anybody with a $10,000 professional/industrial full-bore fax unit and a modem hooked to the Internet, for instance, can send two or three anonymous messages a day to the president(s) of Russia, Brazil or the National Football League that say only, "I LOVE YOU. WHEN CAN WE MEET?" Or, "I AM YOUR BRAIN-DAMAGED BROTHER THAT YOU NEVER KNEW. CALL ME TODAY OR I'LL KILL SOMEBODY."

A lot of fun has been had by fax addicts and warped people. Massive facsimile transmission has also been used by deadly serious people in life-or-death situations. The world would never have known about the 1989 student revolution in China/Tiananmen Square without the fax machines used illegally by students who realized they were about to be run over by tanks. It is, in fact, just about impossible to mount a successful rebellion against anything, these days, unless you have access to at least one safely hidden fax machine that will send your story out to the world.

I HAVE MY OWN checkered history with illegal facsimile transmissions, but there is no need to speak of that now. In fact, most of my work in this medium has been legal and profoundly beneficial. There is a vast spectrum of usage at the high end of the fax culture, and I have tried to use most of it.

There are many queer tricks to it, and most of what I know I have learned from my old friend and fellow techno-hooligan Ed Turner at CNN.

AMENDMENT IV
to the U.S. Constitution

The right of the people to be secure in their persons, houses, papers, and effects, against unreasonable searches and seizures, shall not be violated, and no warrants shall issue, but upon probable cause, supported by oath or affirmation, and particularly describing the place to be searched, and the persons or things to be seized.

Feb 22 '92
Owl Farm

Ed Turner
Executive Vice-president
CNN
Atlanta, GA

Dear Ed,

It's Saturday night and you're giving H. Ross Perot a free hour of national TV time to campaign for president—with his dimwit stooge, Larry King, feeding him lines and cues and setups like one fat grape after another.

I can't stand it, Ed. You are turning CNN into the propaganda arm of the No Fun Club.... Last week(s)/month (almost forever, it seems) you hammered and slurred and terrified millions of innocent women for puffing up their elegant little breasts with silicone implants—just so you and me, Ed, could see them better and notice them quicker and appreciate them more and perhaps want to savor and stroke them from time to time.... And what's wrong with that, Ed? Are you some kind of puritanical body-Nazi? What will you be pushing next week—bundling boards?

Let me gently suggest to you, Ed, that you people are not in a position, as it were, to mount a campaign of repression against high-breasted, ruby-lipped women or hard-working journalists who happen to bounce a check for their bar tabs now and then.... What if you had to fire all the people at CNN who ever bounced a check or had a breast implant?

Yeah. Think what the tabloids could do with that one, Eddie.... Or what the hell? I could maybe do it myself. I'm gearing up to write a "Meltdown in the Media" column for Rolling Stone (every two weeks), and I will have a large staff and a huge budget for tips and information, confidential sources, informants, disgruntled ex-employees, etc. And I know a lot of people in Atlanta.

Where is this new and ominous downdraft of repression coming from—Jane Fonda? Ye gods, Ed. Is that true? Fuck. How could it happen? Yes. I see it all very clearly now....

You'll probably be fired pretty soon, anyway. It will be like dealing with Madam Chiang, once that woman gets her hands on the levers. You'll be hounding me for a job on my research team at R.S. But don't worry, Ed: There will always be a slot for you in my shop.

Yours in Jesus,

HST

02/24/1992 16:33 CNN ADMINISTRATION P.01

CNN

ONE CNN CENTER, Box 105366, Atlanta, GA 30348-5366
(404) 827-1500

FEB 24

HUNTER THOMPSON/MD/SOMEWHERE:

...As to Ms. Fonda nee Turner, it simply is not true that she has taken over CNN. Based on a very brief time in her company, she is too bright to spend much controversial bon mots on we videotape-stained wretches; so what if our correspondents have to jog to stories now instead of taking a cab. What I dread is the discovery that all these satellite dishes cause face zits. That will not be a story well reported here....

By the way, Doc, Jerry Brown is, to me, the most interesting guy in the race. I don't know him well but he is absolutely right on the impact of the campaign big givers on politics. It is not new just more so. He is an unrelenting sort of guy, isn't he? Anyway, our column—Turner & Thompson at Large—must eschew the tired topics of the 60s, 70s, 80s and attack the tired topics of the 90s. The 90s will be the NO FUN DECADE—no booze, no smokes, no sunbathing, no breast balloon-ers, no breathing, no snide jokes, no racial epithets (that's epitaph with a lisp), no breathing, no sex, greed is out and orangy-gooey is in, peo-ple staying at home with their families (sure to lead to more 10 pt type heads MAN SLAUGHTERS ENTIRE FAMILY OF EIGHT). It is up to us to find those in the underground who are keeping sin alive. It's a big job and we can do it. Our first column—Mother Teresa Makes Puppy Chili.

Seize the moment,

ET

Sun	**01 Mar 92**	Senator Brock Adams (WA) retires after sexual allegations
Tue	**03 Mar 92**	George Bush acknowledges in an interview that breaking his "no new taxes" pledge is hurting his reelection campaign, and is thus the biggest mistake of his presidency
Thu	**05 Mar 92**	Kerrey ends race for Democratic nomination
Mon	**09 Mar 92**	Harkin ends presidential campaign
Tue	**10 Mar 92**	Poll before Super Tuesday shows Clinton would beat Bush in a general election For the first time, the *Washington Post*/ABC national poll gives Clinton 46 percent to Bush's 44 percent
Tue	**10 Mar 92**	Clinton and Bush big Super Tuesday winners Clinton wins Florida, Hawaii, Louisiana, Mississippi, Missouri, Oklahoma, Tennessee, Texas. Tsongas wins Massachusetts and Rhode Island. Bush wins overwhelmingly on GOP side, but Buchanan is strong.
Thu	**12 Mar 92**	Democratic delegate count After the March 10 Super Tuesday primaries, the *New York Times* count of national convention delegates is 1,628 of 4,288 Clinton 728 Tsongas 343 Brown 89 Undecided 468
Mon	**16 Mar 92**	Speaking off the cuff to reporters in Chicago, Hillary says, "I suppose I could have stayed home and baked cookies and hot teas. But what I decided to do was pursue my profession, which I entered before my husband was in public life."
Thu	**19 Mar 92**	Paul Tsongas suspends campaign After finishing third in both the Illinois and Michigan primaries, Tsongas suspends his campaign. The former Massachusetts senator says he lacks the funds to continue for the Democratic presidential nomination.
Fri	**20 Mar 92**	Iraq backs down on ballistic missiles
Fri	**20 Mar 92**	Ross Perot announces that he would be willing to spend between $50 million and $100 million of his own money on a run for the presidency
Tue	**24 Mar 92**	Jerry Brown wins Connecticut primary
Fri	**27 Mar 92**	Woman denies having affair with Clinton
Sun	**29 Mar 92**	**Clinton admits he tried pot but did not inhale** **In answer to questions on a local television program in New York City, Clinton admits he had tried smoking marijuana during the time he was a student at Oxford University (1968–70). He says he didn't like pot and has not done it again, adding that he never inhaled.**

MR. BILL'S MARIJUANA PROBLEM: REAL MEN DON'T INHALE

I HAD JUST come back from an incident with the police and a snowmobile when Pat Cadell called from New York, saying that he was with a bunch of *New York Times* reporters in a bar and they were curious to know what I thought about what Clinton had to say about marijuana—that he had tried it in college but "didn't inhale." I was embarrassed. What do you mean "didn't inhale"? What the hell do you think we smoke it for?

I said, "Only a fool would say a thing like that. It's just a disgrace to an entire generation."

My response was printed the next day in the *New York Times*, with a retort from James Carville that said, "I'm sorry the whole reputation of a generation hangs on Bill's inability to breathe in."

Campaign Trail

Hunter Thompson Speaks Out on Bi

Billy Crystal had his say. So did Phil Donahue. Even Regis Philbin found it hard to refrain from commenting when Gov. Bill Clinton insisted that he had never inhaled the marijuana that touched his lips 25 years ago.

So why haven't we heard from the man who carried a black bag filled with drugs on every campaign he ever covered, the man who invented, and perfected, "gonzo" journalism, the missing link between politics and the pharmaceutical industry?

"It's just a disgrace to an entire generation," said Hunter S. Thompson, when asked about Mr. Clinton's decision not to inhale. Mr. Thompson, reached at home in Woody Creek, Colo., was clearly astounded by Mr. Clinton's reserve. But he had to get off the phone in a hurry, he said, because the local police were accusing him of firing a military rocket at a snowmobile.

When informed that Mr. Thompson would, in all probability, not support Mr. Clinton, one of the candidate's chief strategists seemed dismayed.

"I'm sorry the whole reputation of a generation hangs on Bill's inability to breathe in," James Carville said. "It could weigh kind of heavy on him."

A Ceremonial Toss Ends in the Dirt

Remember George Bush?

With no opponent in the New York primary, the President has been free to visit more contested regions, depositing Federal money, housing projects and choice Government sinecures like a latter-day Johnny Appleseed spreading political bounty.

Yesterday he turned up at the opening of the new Baltimore baseball stadium, determined to absorb some free publicity and perhaps repair his emerging reputation as a guy who cannot get a ball over the plate.

Forgetaboutit. With 48,000 fans as witnesses, the 67-year-old former captain of the Yale baseball team ditched the opening pitch into the dirt for the second year in a row.

"I don't want to just get it to the plate," said the confident President before the big event. "The pros tell me that a lot of amateurs go out and they throw it into the dirt even though they have great arms."

After the ceremonial toss fell short, Mr. Bush said, more sheepishly, "I thought I was up against Ted Williams."

Then he added, "What I mean is, it just ran out of gas."

How Not to Run For President I

How not to run for President I:

Ho, ho, I thought. Good old James. He is very fast on his feet—unlike Mr. Bill—and that's why they pay him big money to tell candidates what to say to the *New York Times* when dope addicts on the press bus start asking dumb questions.

Q–"*Why* didn't you inhale, Governor?"

A–"What? Could you repeat the question?"

(confused scuffling as Carville seizes the mike)

Carville–"What the Governor means is that he never inhales *anything*, because of his asthma condition. He can only breath *out*, not in."

Q–"Is that true, Governor?"

A–"Let's clear it up right now. The answer to your rude and stupid question is that I can't inhale and I will never cum in your mouth."

Q–"What? Could you say that again, Governor?"

A–(Carville interrupts) "Never mind that, Bubba. What the Governor means is that he gave up smoking and sex and a lot of other things when he made the decision to run for president. Any more questions? Okay. Thank you very much. See you at Plato's Retreat."

---

ll Clinton and Marijuana

Known for campaigning more with a whimper than a bang, Edmund G. Brown Jr. ended his assault on New York voters last evening with a vigorous rally at Brooklyn's Borough Hall.

It was one of the few events that Mr. Brown's staff has scheduled explicitly in time to appear on the nighly news, and the plan might have worked if the candidate's entire national press contingent had not lost its way in the Bronx.

"We landed at La Guardia and got on the bus," said one of the many reporters who spent the late afternoon on an unscheduled tour of some of the nation's poorest urban areas. "We were supposed to follow a lead car. They had no idea where they were."

How Not to Run For President II

How not to run for President II: Bill Clinton, in fullest man-of-the-people mode, goes to Brooklyn.

First stop, Flatbush. After about 30 minutes of casually strolling, with a police helicopter hovering above and a knot of hecklers shouting such New York greetings as "Bill Clinton is a Klansman," the candidate's 15-car motorcade starts to crawl toward his next stop in Bushwick.

Suddenly, the whole caravan lurches to a halt. Nervous reporters and campaign aides jump out of their cars and start racing toward the Governor, fearing the worst.

Police sirens cut the air, red lights flash wildly and dozens of children run forward shouting: "It's a riot! It's a riot!"

"What happened? What happened?" wild-eyed reporters demand to know.

"Never mind," a tired aide replies. "He just saw somebody from Arkansas and jumped out to say hi."

Somebody from Arkansas. In Bushwick?

MICHAEL SPECTER

The Primary In New York

Only Democrats enrolled by March 13 can vote in the New York Presidential primary today. There is no Republican primary.

Nominations for the United States Senate, House of Representatives, the Legislature and other offices will be decided by primaries in September.

Polls are open from 6 A.M. to 9 P.M. in New York City, Nassau, Suffolk, Westchester, Rockland, Orange, Ulster and Erie Counties, and from noon to 9 P.M. elsewhere in the state.

Voters with questions may call 212-NYC-VOTE in New York City, or county election boards.

THAT IS CARVILLE'S JOB, whether he's working for the next president of the United States or the one-term governor of New Jersey. Some days you win big with gibberish and on some days you lose a 22-point lead in the blink of an eye when your opponent outsmarts you by giving fistfuls of $100 bills to black preachers in Newark, to make sure negroes won't vote.

(That is what happened to poor James in a major gubernatorial race, not long after Clinton became president. At least that's how Ed Rollins told it to the press.) Okay, back to business. Bill Clinton does not inhale marijuana, right? You bet. Like I chew on LSD but I don't swallow it. And Richard Nixon was not a crook.... Which is technically true. Nixon was never *convicted* of anything. He resigned for reasons of his own. He was getting too nervous to be president any longer, so he "did the right thing" by turning the Oval Office over to vice president Gerald Ford, in exchange for a presidential pardon.... Ford wept as Nixon was taken away, but he knew in his heart that he was doing a far, far better thing than he had ever done before. By accepting the burden of the presidency, he would set Richard Nixon free to pursue peace all over the world.

Even children laughed, but it worked. They all got rich in the end. And ex-Soviet premier Nikita Khrushchev—who once said that "sending Nixon to a peace conference is like sending a goat to tend the cabbages"—is still spinning in his grave.

This is the way it works in big-time politics. Deny everything. Never plead guilty. What marijuana? Fuck you, I'm innocent, and you're not....

Wed 01 Apr 92	Syndicated TV talk-show host Phil Donahue drills Clinton about an alleged affair with Gennifer Flowers and draft evasion. Clinton: "I don't think it's an example of bad character to admit you're not perfect." Refusing to answer questions about Flowers, Clinton tells Donahue if his line of questioning doesn't stop, "We're going to sit here in a lot of silence, Phil."
Tue 07 Apr 92	PLO leader Arafat survives crash landing in desert
Wed 08 Apr 92	Arthur Ashe reveals AIDS infection
Thu 09 Apr 92	Federal grand jury charges House post office clerk with embezzling and drug dealing

Which is usually true, in this league. It was Adolf Hitler who got credit for saying "a lie repeated often enough becomes the truth." (Probably it was Winston Churchill who said that, or maybe Franklin Roosevelt. Who knows? Churchill was a natural-born liar, and Roosevelt was a serious paraplegic who won four straight campaigns for the presidency of the United States while sitting in a wheelchair that was never mentioned to the voters. It was like Michael Jordan winning the NBA scoring title for six straight years while using a wooden leg, or Stephen Hawking winning a sprint medal in the Olympics.)

The moral of this story is that more people in wheelchairs should run for president—along with dope smokers who don't inhale and sex fiends who gave up sex for politics.

No. Scratch that. There is no room in the politics business for morality tales, and Bill Clinton understands this just as keenly as any other successful politician. He gained ten points in New Hampshire by flat-out *denying* the same "sex, drugs, and rock 'n' roll" charges Gary Hart admitted to four years earlier that sent him from the White House to the outhouse in 10 days.

That is the *real* lesson of presidential politics in the nineties. Never admit anything, except where you were born. *Of course* Bill Clinton never inhaled when he put the bong to his lips. *Of course* he never knew Gennifer Flowers. *Of course* he never beat Chelsea for not eating her turnips at fund-raisers.... Why should he? What the fuck? He is, after all, the President. And the President never acts weird. That is the way it works, Bubba. Ask Richard Nixon. Or Jack Kennedy—who acted so weird in the White House that the first thing Nixon did, when he took over in '68, was have the White House swimming pool filled up with concrete and turned into a million-pound slab/base for what is now the pressroom. Jack Kennedy never inhaled, and neither did Marilyn Monroe. Not even when they were swimming naked and snorting cocaine on the diving board. Hell no. Why should they? They were smart people, and smart people don't inhale. Not if they want to be elected. That is all ye know, Bubba, and all ye need to know.

Wed	**22 Apr 92**	Duke abandons race for Republican nomination

Sun	**26 Apr 92**	National polls show three-way race: Bush/Clinton/Perot Bush 38% Clinton 28% Perot 23%
Mon	**27 Apr 92**	Jackson demands VP nomination The New York *Daily News* quotes Jesse Jackson as saying, "If I am rejected this time, I am prepared to react"
Tue	**28 Apr 92**	Bush wins Pennsylvania and nomination delegate votes: Democrats: Clinton 57%, Brown 26%, Tsongas 13% Republicans: Bush 27%, Buchanan 23%
Wed	**29 Apr 92**	Following a jury verdict acquitting four policemen of assault in the videotaped beating of Rodney King, rioting erupts in Los Angeles
Wed	**06 May 92**	CA poll shows Perot leading in general election
Sun	**17 May 92**	Results from a CNN/*Time* survey show that in a three-way race, Perot would receive 33 percent, Bush 28 percent, Clinton 24 percent
Tue	**19 May 92**	Dan Quayle denounces Murphy Brown
Fri	**22 May 92**	Bush press secretary Marlin Fitzwater calls Ross Perot a "monster," adding that he thinks Perot is "dangerous"
Tue	**02 Jun 92**	Primary season ends with Bush and Clinton winning needed delegates
Wed	**03 Jun 92**	Perot hires top strategists to manage campaign—Ed Rollins, Reagan's '84 campaign director, and Hamilton Jordan, Carter's '76 manager
Wed	**03 Jun 92**	**Clinton plays sax on late-night TV**

CARPE DIEM: DOING THE WRONG THING FOR THE RIGHT REASONS

AND THEN it occurred to me: What about the rock 'n' roll vote? There was a lot of arrogance in Bill Clinton and I wondered if he would backhand the rock 'n' roll vote. Shit, we have more votes than Jesse Jackson. Why don't we invite the three candidates to meet the *Rolling Stone* editorial board? Like the *Washington Post* and *New York Times.* Fuck 'em, we have a bigger vote than they do.

June 3, 1992

To: Jann... c.c. Bill Greider, P. J. O'Rourke, Pat Caddell

Hot damn. We're back into politics again. And why not? If a whining newt like Rich Bond can be the chairman of the Republican National Committee, and if Ron Brown speaks for the Democrats—shit, it is time for the National Affairs Desk to get cranked up again, for good or ill, and sure as hell not for long.... But what the fuck? You know how me and Mother Nature feel about vacuums.... Right. We abhor them, and it is somehow our job to fill them, because otherwise things will implode and go boom and wander sideways at top speed and be sucked back and forth right in front of our eyes like greasy rolling cannons sucked loose from all their moorings and crash around like bombs on the increasingly slick and slanted decks of our own lives.

Well, well, well—let's suck that one back up on our monitor again, and have another look at it....

Right. We do have a choice, but not really. If it's true—and I think it is—that politics is the art of controlling your environment, then now is the time to get seriously into politics.... Because if we don't, somebody else will, and they probably won't be on our side.

Ah, but who is our side? Who is us? That is the question—or at least a big part of it. Maybe there is no rock 'n' roll vote. But I think there could be, if we wanted to put it together.

Why not? Jesse Jackson has bodies, but we have votes... maybe (if the bodies vote), and I think we can make that happen; or at least we can threaten the lizard-bastards with it and maybe force them into a few commitments, like Jesse tries to do.

But, shit—we are bigger than Jesse, and our demands are far less complex. All we want is a total commitment to Amendments I and IV of the U.S. Constitution: free speech and privacy.

Why not? Let's make the bastards explain why not. Let's take the high road and force them down to the low one if they won't agree with us.

Who the fuck would vote for a presidential candidate who was against free speech and the right to privacy?

Not me, Bubba. And not you, either, eh? Hell no! Let's make these fuckers come to the Rolling Stone forum and answer these questions on big-time national TV.

Yes. We are the voice of rock 'n' roll, and we are legion. Stand back! We don't need no stinkin' badges. And—if we stand together (yeah, there's always a catch)—you can't get elected without us. We are the 20-million-pound-vote gorilla, and we will sit wherever we fucking want to.

Okay for now. Send money at once. I can't sustain this level of political warfare without cash.

Thu	**11 Jun 92**	Clinton campaign staff forgoes paychecks
Thu	**11 Jun 92**	Congress defeats Balanced Budget Amendment
Thu	**11 Jun 92**	Bush tear-gassed in Panama
Sat	**13 Jun 92**	Speaking to Jesse Jackson's Rainbow Coalition, Clinton attacks rap singer Sister Souljah for using racially inflammatory language in a recent *Washington Post* interview
Mon	**15 Jun 92**	While watching a Trenton, New Jersey, school spelling bee, Dan Quayle miscorrects the spelling of *potato* a 12-year-old had put on the blackboard. Quayle insists that the word has an *e* on it.
Tue	**16 Jun 92**	Caspar Weinberger indicted

Thu	**18 Jun 92**	Jackson denounces Clinton's attack on rap singer as having "again exposed a character flaw"
Sun	**21 Jun 92**	*Washington Post* reports Perot investigated Bush

To: Playboy

June 24, 1992

Owl Farm

"Too many whores."

This is a hard one to call—especially from 10,000 miles away and 8,000 feet high and 19 weeks before the election. . . . But what the hell. We are, after all, professionals, and we do our finest work, our highest and keenest thinking, under conditions of extreme pressure.

Ho, ho. So try this: Only a fool would vote this year. The smart people will hunker down like dazed rabbits—quivering and staring and shitting on each other while they hop back and forth in their cages. The smart will ignore politics this year. They will pretend to be dumb, like the bunny-rabbit, but they will really be acting smart.

Shit on them, that's what I say. Let them burrow deep like moles. In fact they are dumber than moles, and many will be dyed bright yellow before Election Day. . . . How's that for an image? All smart people dyed yellow. Or maybe pink. Who knows? They are doomed.

Pink is the color of stupid, and yellow is the color of dumb. There are too many whores in politics these days, but the night of the whore-hopper is coming. Many will be called, and 9 out of 10 will be chosen—to be herded down the long, slippery ramp and into the bottomless sheep dip, where they will wallow and struggle helplessly (some of them drowning), until their bodies are disinfected by powerful acids, vapors and the fumes of terrible lice medicines that will fry their brains like bacon left too long in the microwave. Ronald Reagan was right, back in the winter of '85, when he told a reporter from People that Armageddon is now and that "this generation may be the one that will have to face the end of the world."

Well... maybe so, Bubba, maybe so. But I'll believe it when I see it. Those bastards have been promising us the apocalypse for as far back as I can remember, but they always weasel out of it—and, frankly, I've just about given up hope. Fuck them. They lie. Hell, it's worse than a roofing and siding racket, or some kind of Ponzi scheme.

No. We will not be that lucky. The end will not come quickly, like it says in Revelation 22:7. First will come the shit-rain, then the sheep dip, and after that, the terrible night of the whore-hopper, which might last for 1,000 years.

"And when the thousand years are expired, Satan shall be loosed out of his prison."

That's Revelation 20:7, which is only the tip of the iceberg. The bad news comes in the last two verses of chapter 20—14 and 15—where it says:

"And death and hell were cast into the lake of fire. This is the second death. And whosoever was not found written in the book of life was cast into the lake of fire."

Yeah. And how's that for a sneak preview of your golden years? Cast into the lake of fire, with Satan clawing at your legs and trying to drag you under....

Horrible, horrible. It is a grim prospect for Jesus freaks, because they know the Bible says that Satan is a cross between a crocodile and a huge hyena. He has seven heads and 600 teeth and he weighs 1,000 pounds—a nasty thing to feel getting hold of your leg when you're trying to stay afloat in a lake of fire.

That is what a vote for Ross Perot will get you. And a vote for George Bush will get you "cast into the great winepress of the wrath of God," which is more or less where we are now, if you believe what you read in the newspapers.

So that leaves Clinton, I guess.... Yeah, good old Bill. At least he plays the skin flute, and he doesn't mind ducking behind a hedge now and then for a bit of the suckee-suckee in the course of his afternoon jog.

The Bible also says, "The tortoise shall overtake the hare, then kill him and eat him."

So who are we to argue? The fat is in the fire.... This ain't no normal election year. A man would have to be crazy not to hit the streets with his vote in his hand on November 3, if only to cast it where it can do the most damage—preferably to George Bush. Why not? It may be the last fun we'll have for a while. Death to the weird.

Wed	**24 Jun 92**	**Perot accuses Bush of dirty tricks**
Sun	**28 Jun 92**	Baboon's liver implanted in terminally ill man
Mon	**29 Jun 92**	The U.S. Supreme Court reaffirms the right-to-abortion decision over Pennsylvania law, but approves parts of law restricting abortion
Tue	**30 Jun 92**	*Washington Post* publishes poll in three-way race: Bush 36%, Clinton 29%, Perot 26%
Wed	**01 Jul 92**	Bush exonerated in hostage-release inquiry
Wed	**01 Jul 92**	First food airlifted to Sarajevo
Sun	**05 Jul 92**	***New York Times* reports Perot tried to influence Reagan White House in MIA negotiations**

CHAPTER 5

JULY: The Nightmare of Ross Perot

A pig will walk in the wilderness,
a pig will walk on the sea.
A pig will walk wherever he wants,
but no pig walks on me.

— F. X. Leach, Iowa City, 1986

THE WOMAN WAS almost dead when we brought her back to headquarters, but Sonny said she would live. We stood back while he rolled her over on her stomach and stepped on her back to make her start breathing again, then he lit a cigarette and tossed it on her back. She jumped and began coughing. He stepped on her back again, and she began snoring harshly.

"My god! What's wrong with her?" shouted one of the staff lawyers.

"Nothing," said Sonny. "She's ready to go on TV."

"O god *no*!" screamed the lawyer. "Not with the *candidate*! We'll all go to prison!"

"Bullshit," said Sonny. "She's with Ross." Right. Welcome to Club '90. The world ain't what it used to be—and before this thing is over, you'll wish that you weren't either.... The snake has swallowed the chicken, Bubba, and the only place to hide is a different name to call it.

Indeed. I just got a call from my old friend Frank Mankiewicz, who says that Ross Perot has begun to grow a thin blond mustache on his upper lip—to the horror of his new top advisors, Hamilton Jordan and Ed Rollins, who feel it will queer his image. Other key staffers, including Consigliere Tom Luce and Propaganda Minister James Squires, have tried to put a good face, as it were, on the candidate's new facial hair—calling it "love moss" and "intellectual growth."

Ho, ho. "That's what Adolf said just before the Night of the Long Knives," said Mankiewicz, now a senior vice president of Hill and Knowlton, the heaviest of all political image-makers.

"You watch," said Mankiewicz. "He will cultivate the mustache very slowly, and his people will deny it's happening for as long as possible—but when the cold winds blow in November, it will be there. It will be a stiff, short little brush, and Jordan will call a press conference to explain that he knew 'Ross had a mustache from the very beginning.' And Rollins will call for the arrest and no-bail imprisonment of all the 'rotten, anti-American bigots who hate the sight of facial hair.'"

Tue **07 Jul 92** Quayle alludes to Slick Willy

Speaking in New York, Quayle says, "One reason George Bush will win this election is that the American people know his character: He is honest, not slick; he offers leadership, he doesn't pander to special interest; and he is willing to stand up for basic values, rather than treating all lifestyle choices as morally equivalent."

ROSS PEROT SPEAKS:

Dilettante politics in the nineties...
A new kind of fun-hog shows up at the O.K. Corral...
Beware: You have been warned...

ROSS PEROT was the best thing that happened in American politics since Richard Nixon acquired a taste for gin. In both cases, the political dialogue of the day was enriched by spontaneous gibberish that entertained the wrong people and made the right ones question their faith.

When Nixon appeared suddenly on TV to announce that he'd decided to abandon the war in Vietnam and surrender honorably to the Vietcong, the stock market almost crashed and caravans of frightened superpatriots began moving toward the mountains of Idaho, north Georgia and Arkansas, where others of their kind were busy building forts and burying stolen guns and teaching their children to speak Chinese.

Perot's whimsical decision to run for President of the United States had the same kind of galvanizing effect on tens of thousands of closet politics junkies in 1992. They didn't like Bush, Clinton or anyone else on the ballot that year, but when Perot tossed his hat in the ring, they rallied behind him like lemmings and swore to fight to the death for Ross, because he seemed to speak for them.

Ho, ho.

IT WAS ROSS PEROT'S bizarre candidacy that first really got me into the 1992 campaign. If Ross hadn't slithered into the race, I would never have been there either. Bill Clinton had never impressed me, and George Bush was a criminal fraud worse than Nixon. It was like a choice between a Leech and a Gila Monster, a no-win situation and a fine opportunity to escape my addiction and seek a different way of life. With all the candidates being losers, bums and degenerates, it was a good year to get out of the politics business.

Which I did, for a while: I quit and felt clean about it, despite a constant barrage of temptation and phone calls from old friends who tried to lure me into the fray—usually for their own reasons, and I knew they were wrong....

So when I fell off the wagon, I did it quick, like any other junkie—and it was Ross Perot, not Clinton, who made me do it. Yeah, good old Ross. At first he looked like fun—not because he might win, but because he might prevent either Clinton or Bush from winning and throw the 1992 presidential election into the U.S. House of Representatives and certain chaos, which appealed to me very strongly at the time. It is awkward for me to admit, now, that the fun I saw with Perot was not democracy, but anarchy.

Probably I was just looking for some action, but my mother diagnosed it as paranoid psychosis and said she was feeling it too. "They think we're stupid," she said. "Do you know that the suicide rate among smart people goes up like a rocket in presidential election years? It jumps about 40 percent, just like clockwork, every four years."

"Where did you get that?" I asked her.

"From the Statistical Abstract of the United States," she said. "I know exactly what I'm talking about."

I was stunned. It was true, and I hated it. "You crazy old bitch!" I screamed. "You talk like Ross Perot! Get out of my face!"

She laughed and changed the subject. "I hear you're going to vote for Perot," she said.

"Not necessarily. I'm going to be a Perot delegate to the electoral college, but I won't vote for him."

THAT WAS MY PLAN, and it made perfect sense, at the time. It was the only way to get involved in a presidential election that otherwise seemed to be a meaningless drill with no sense of possibility or passion.

You didn't have to be a campaign junkie to feel a sense of loss and melancholy at the prospect of a Bush/Quayle vs. Clinton/Gore superbowl in 1992. It looked like a rerun of '76: Another self-righteous, New Age, boll-weevil Southern Democrat against another greedy dimwit, corrupt, caretaker Republican.

Fuck that, I thought. Look what happened last time. Alas, poor Jimmy, I knew him well....

Indeed. Easy come, easy go. And some people will tell you that the GOP brain trust didn't really mind losing to Carter anyway. They were already bogged down in the disgrace of Watergate and Nixon's grim legacy, and Gerald Ford was not the kind of champion who would lead them out of the wilderness and back to respectability. No. It was better to lay low for a while and regroup for 1980, when Ronald Reagan would be ready. And it worked.

There is no such thing as paranoia in a presidential campaign. Anything you fear or suspect will almost always turn out to be true, and the fix is always in, somewhere, and the enemy of your enemy is not always your friend. And that, for the true campaign junkie, is precisely what makes it fun. The act never speaks for itself. *Non res ipsa loquitor.*

So there was nothing stupid or strange in the notion—which occurred to me early on—that whatever passed for the GOP brain trust after Lee Atwater died might decide to go into the tank again, in 1992. After all, it looked like a good year to duck out of the White House and avoid being held responsible for the collapse of the national economy—and if George Bush had a problem with going down in history as a failed, one-term president, so what? He was never in charge anyway, and his ego was expendable. It was a far, far better thing, in the long run, for George to take a fall in '92 than to have the whole party sent to the guillotine in '96. You bet. Look what happened the last time a Republican president tried to fix a doomed national economy. Remember Herbert Hoover?

James Baker III said that, as I recall. Or maybe it was Robert Dole. Either way, the logic was compelling, and it took a lot of zip out of the warrior spirit on both sides. The last thing any campaign junkie needs to think is that the election is fixed even before the first votes are counted in New Hampshire. That *really* takes the fun out of it.

It was also what made Ross Perot interesting, at least to people like me. With Bush stumbling and Clinton constantly tripping over his own dick, a maverick third-party spoiler like Perot might whip up a serious "antipolitics" frenzy and prevent anybody from getting the required 270 electoral votes. And when that happened, things would start to unravel at high speed.

Hot damn, I thought at the time, I want to be in on this. I was, after all, a professional, and what better way to get the story of a presidential election run amok than to be a suddenly empowered voting member of the electoral college, where I would not necessarily have to cast my vote for the candidate I was pledged to. It was clearly the opportunity of a lifetime for anybody who believes—as I do, for good or ill—that aggressive political action can be a very effective way of controlling your environment in a democracy. It was also an invitation to participate in what would surely be a gigantic political scam, a high-stakes orgy of vote-peddling, back-stabbing and treachery that would cancel the election results and leave the electors free to choose their own president. It was irresistible.

I called Democratic headquarters immediately, but their 26 electoral college slots from Colorado were already filled. I got the same story from GOP headquarters, even though I was a certified member of the Republican Presidential Task Force. Clearly, I was not the first campaign junkie to see this option and grab for it.

My last hope was a call to Perot headquarters, where I was surprised to find that not all of their EC slots were yet filled. "Wonderful," I said. "Pencil me in. I've been on your side from the start."

They seemed pleased, and so was I for a while, but it didn't last long. The trouble came when I was asked to sign an undated letter of resignation *before* being given the job. "That's the way Mr. Perot wants it," they said. "And that's the way it is."

Which was true. The clever little bastard had closed the only remaining loophole. At the first hint of disloyalty, Perot would fire me by accepting my "resignation." Welcome to the nineties, Bubba. I told you it was wrong.

IN THE MIDDLE of all this, I was persudaded to hold a traditional family-style Fourth of July party, which was somehow a stunning success—despite a savage invasion by a gang of local thugs, parolees and degenerates who arrived around noon, with no warning, on a flock of noisy, rich-looking Harleys that jammed up the driveway and terrified the girls....

But not for long. I called the police and had them all arrested for trespassing and public drunkenness. A few resisted and were beaten severely. Then my naked friend, Jilly, got on my tractor and crushed their motorcycles, ramming them repeatedly at high speed with a three-ton rock-crusher attached to the front of my supercharged turbojet 16-geared John Deere 770SST/Magnum Twin-Rhino earth-mover.

Ed Bradley was reading the Declaration of Independence to a group of children on the front porch at the time, and he paid no attention to the nightmare of carnage and police brutality happening in the driveway. One of the hoodlums got crushed under his own Knucklehead and later had to have his legs amputated.

So what? I thought. I was tired of these filthy-rich thugs

from Planet Hollywood. They ride like old women and can't hold their liquor. They will never understand the kind of high-white, otherworldly grace that comes with whipping around a blind, downhill, half-wet corner into a wall of huge eucalyptus trees at 155 miles an hour with a Peterbilt suddenly looming out of the fog in the oncoming lane and kind of wavering out there in the long thin beam of your headlight....

Ah, but never mind that morbid, freaky kind of thinking, eh? I'm a BMW man, myself—but what the hell? I gave up riding in gangs a long time ago, and anything that you can drive with one hand at night on a two-lane road at 90 miles an hour in fourth gear is about as fast as I need, these days....

Almost any fool can crank a big bike up to 180 or so—but slowing the bastard down on a diminishing-radius curve into some greasy little freeway is a whole different gig.

Ah, memories, memories: How heavy and crazy they seem on a lonely Friday night when the only real action straight out in front of you is the specter of having to choose whether George Bush or Bill Clinton or Ross Perot will be more or less running your life for the next 4 or 9 or 19 years, or maybe for as long as you live.

CRUNCH TIME IN NEW YORK

The coming of Mr. Bill, and first riffs in the seduction of the rock 'n' roll vote...The assassination of Ross Perot...Ducking out of the convention...Further adventures of Ed Rollins...

NOBODY SANE goes to a national political convention unless they get paid for it, or get an offer they can't refuse. I had both of these, but even then I said no. Like William Faulkner replied when asked why he turned down an invitation to have dinner in the White House with John Kennedy, it was "just too far to go and I hate crowds." Faulkner was teaching at the University of Virginia at the time, only a two-hour drive from Washington—but for me it was 2,000 miles, so I figured I had a good excuse. Besides, I had a ticket to Dallas for a meeting with Ross Perot, who at the time seemed a lot more interesting than anybody likely to emerge from the Demo convention in New York. He still looked like a spoiler. Polls in California showed him leading both Clinton and Bush by huge margins, making him the front-runner in a state that nobody with a real-

Thu	09 Jul 92	**Senator Al Gore named as vice presidential running mate**
Fri	10 Jul 92	*Time* magazine poll shows public doubts about economy
Sat	11 Jul 92	Perot offends NAACP—refers to audience as "you people"
Mon	13 Jul 92	**Democratic National Convention opens in New York**

istic chance at the presidency can afford to lose. Perot had also bolstered his campaign staff by hiring my old friend Hamilton Jordan and veteran GOP wizard Ed Rollins as co–campaign managers. As a gambler, I saw Ross as a viable dark-horse bet, and I'd already received a few feelers about taking the second spot on the ticket with him. I was flattered, but it was clearly out of the question. My attorneys warned me that I wouldn't last three days under the brutal glare of media exposure lifestyle questions that would be inevitable if I caved in to my sense of obligation to the burden of public service.

"You'll be in prison before Christmas," said one, "even if you are innocent."

IT WAS GOOD advice and I took it. Perot stunned the world by suddenly *dropping out* of the race, muttering darkly about strangers threatening to flood the nation with pornographic photos of his daughter if he didn't quit immediately, which he did—and nobody ever even asked him what the hell he was talking about. A skin magazine in New York claimed to have the alleged photos but had decided for reasons of conscience not to publish them, because they were "just too horrible," and that was never explained either. I had a few calls from sources who said they could get the photos for me, if they existed, but I never got back to them. It was a road too low, as they say, and I had better things to do.

Wed	**15 Jul 92**	Benign tumor removed from pope's colon
Wed	**15 Jul 92**	**Ed Rollins announces he is leaving the Perot campaign**
Wed	**15 Jul 92**	Democratic convention nominates Bill Clinton as the presidential candidate
Thu	**16 Jul 92**	**Perot quits presidential race**

Billy Kimball/Comedy Central

Attn: Al Franken

Dear Billy:

Thanx for your kind invitation to comment on the vaguely wretched convention that you people just endured—but I spent most of the week bogged down in negotiations in Dallas with Ross Perot about the VP slot; and then all of a sudden around dawn on Wednesday they cut off all the telephones, and every door in the building slammed shut with big magnets that none of our personal computer keys would fit anymore, and people were starting to panic and whimper and scream at each other about maybe Ross was being assassinated in one of the secret elevators by either Ed Rollins or Hamilton Jordan or maybe thugs in the pay of Neil Bush.

And then all the fucking lights went out for 30 or 40 seconds, and I felt somebody grab me from behind and cut off my wind while the lights kept flickering, and all of the goddamn smoke detectors started going off, and I had a sense of dying stupidly in some kind of horrible, high-tech frenzy with people all around me screaming, Ross! Ross! O god please help me, Ross!

Jesus. It lasted for three or four hours or maybe even <u>days</u> while they were torturing Rollins until he gave up the codes that he tried to sneak out with, and when they grabbed him he was trying to transmit them on some kind of secret wireless modem that he'd stolen out of Ross's personal safe and was trying to hook up to his poor wife in Bali, where he'd sent her to hide out after she "quit" her job in the White House and tried to act like an innocent victim of Ed's political bungling and just needed a separate vacation in Bali for a while so she wouldn't have to think about politics or the ash heap of her personal career....

Ho, ho, ho. So long, Ed. And sorry about your wife. We found her out there on the crayfish flats, not long after dawn, still clutching her personal top-secret White House computer codebook, no bigger than a package of Class B Djarum-Kretek clove/Indo cigarettes.

How horrible. Who would have thought it? The Rollinses were a political couple. Honorable people.

WELL...SHUCKS. What can I say? Except *never mind* that election-night party we were talking about. We guessed wrong, once again....Yeah: Perot just quit. *Whacko.* Just like that. Zip! Gone! Finished! No more Mr. Citizen.

The hog is out of the tunnel. The fat that went into the fire about 88 days ago has now disappeared in a stupid little sizzle and a blip of greasy smoke.

Yeah. Good ole Ross. That wretched, shit-eating little swine. He is like the groundhog. He came out of his goddamn high-tech little hole and took one look around him and understood at once that there were, indeed, many shadows. And they were not his.

No. They were huge. And they moved at terrible speeds, but spoke only gibberish.

I was cranking up for some kind of king-hell atavistic endeavor—like we knew in the good old days, when we howled and jabbered and bounced around the room all night long like human golf balls every time the numbers came in from weird places like Pensacola and Butte and Sacramento, and the balance would swing back and forth....

That *might* happen this time—but it won't come anywhere near the kind of craziness that was guaranteed to happen with a three-way race.

Forget the House of Representatives. That was pie in the sky. They were only fucking with us, Bubba, and now they are going to fuck with Citizen Ross Perot....You bet. Remember Lyndon LaRouche? Two hundred and thirty-seven federal marshalls descended on his house one day, and he was never seen again. Seven consecutive life terms for fraud, stupidity and hubris....

Sorry. We almost had our hands on it—but they double-crossed us once again. Politicians. Shit on them. Good luck, Bubba. It's every man for himself now.

Sun **26 Jul 92** *Chicago Tribune* editorial calls for Quayle to leave Republican ticket

Wed 22 Jul 92	Bush/Quayle deny Quayle-less ticket
Wed 22 Jul 92 to Thu 23 Jul 92	Quayle contradicts Republicans' abortion platform When given a "what if" about his daughter when she grew up, the VP states he would support her decision re pregnancy. Marilyn states the following day that this was not true. Their daughter would in any situation carry to full term.

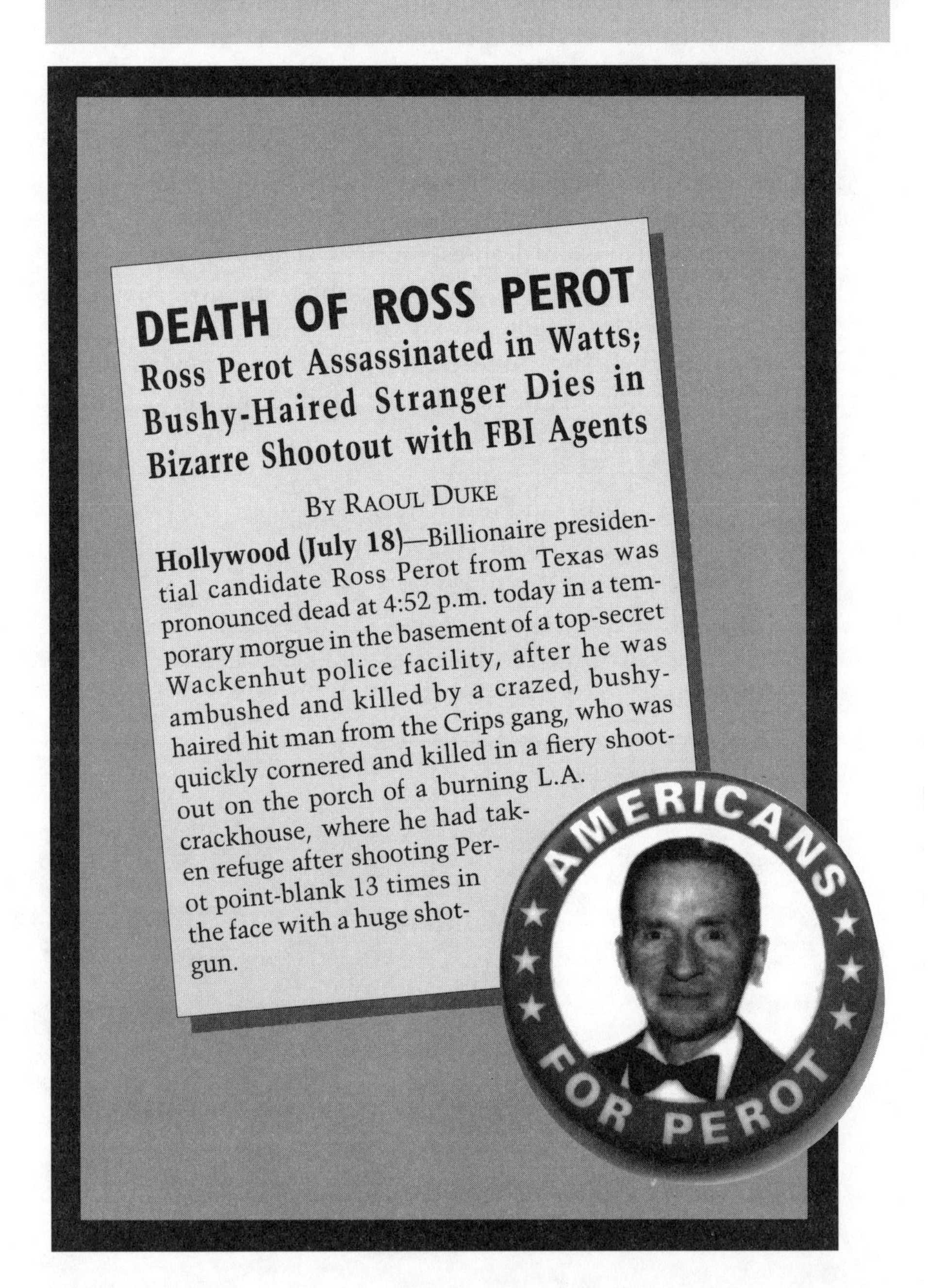

DEATH OF ROSS PEROT

Ross Perot Assassinated in Watts; Bushy-Haired Stranger Dies in Bizarre Shootout with FBI Agents

BY RAOUL DUKE

Hollywood (July 18)—Billionaire presidential candidate Ross Perot from Texas was pronounced dead at 4:52 p.m. today in a temporary morgue in the basement of a top-secret Wackenhut police facility, after he was ambushed and killed by a crazed, bushy-haired hit man from the Crips gang, who was quickly cornered and killed in a fiery shootout on the porch of a burning L.A. crackhouse, where he had taken refuge after shooting Perot point-blank 13 times in the face with a huge shotgun.

CHAPTER 6

THE DEATH OF FUN: Welcome to Little Rock

The Four Stooges meet the next president...Memo from the National Affairs Desk, July 22...

July 22, 1992

MEMO FROM THE NATIONAL AFFAIRS DESK #222

TO: Jann Wenner / Editorial

FROM: Dr. Thompson

SUBJECT: Welcome to the end of the American Century—Politics '92, bad wreck in the fast lane, bad news for fun-hogs.... The treachery of Ross Perot, the sleaziness of George Bush and the end of the world as we know it.... Welcome to Mr. Bill's Neighborhood: Lay low, act dumb, and prepare for the night of the whore-hopper....

We live in hideous times, Jann. The nineties will go down in history as one of those nasty little backwaters when bad things happened to dumb people and things went wrong and nobody cared and nobody laughed and fear was the governing ethic.

People will not want to read about what happened to us "back in the nineties." It will be too depressing, too grim, at least for Americans. And that's us, Bubba. Yeah, you and me, the boys from the Bop-Kabala. Yes, we're the chosen ones, Jann. History has chosen us to speak for our times and our people. If we don't, somebody else will, and they will be vicious like rats and hyenas, and they will probably not be on our side.

Ross Perot was only the first of them—the New Age political predators—Perot is a greedy little dingbat with no balls at all, who was a charlatan from the very beginning. H. L. Mencken would have loved him. He is a monument to Mencken's dictum that says, "Every third American devotes himself to improving and uplifting his fellow citizen, usually by force." Ross Perot fits that description in spades, but so what? He is a tiny little ferret of a man with a genius for marketing gimmicks and an eerie basic resemblance to a man they called Adolf Hitler. . . .

It made a lot of people nervous, and frankly, I was one of them.

It wasn't just Ross that was dangerous. It was the way he emerged out of nowhere and became a dark-horse favorite to win a three-way election and become the president of the United States. One day he was just another Dallas billionaire and the next he was the American dream.

It was Henry Luce, they say, who first proclaimed in public that this century—the 20th—was in fact the American century, and our fate was to rule the world, whether we wanted to or not. We had no choice, he said. It was our manifest destiny, our role in the great scheme of history. And besides, it was also God's will.

That was good enough for most people (God was very big back then, and nobody wanted to cross Him)—but it was not good enough for the Japs or the Germans or the Chinks or the brutal Italian fascisti who worked for Mussolini when he decided to annex Africa.

This is the end of a century, which has always been known as the Decadence. And it is the end of the American century.

FOURTH AMENDMENT FOUNDATION
405 South Presa Street
San Antonio, Texas 78205-3495

Sent to N. Hollander
7/27/92 3:05pm

July 27, 1992

Nancy Hollander, Esq.
President NACDL
20 First Plaza
Albuquerque, NM
87102

Dear Nancy,

There are, as you know, those among us of exceeding little faith, in re my promised due diligence in our Fourth Amendment Foundation wars. They are sluggards and lechers and degenerates, and they have been a terrible albatross around my neck for many months.... Indeed, we know these people, and they are doomed to know themselves for what they are.

Thank God for you, Nancy. You have been a pillar of strength in a peat bog of weak reeds.... And now I ask your assistance, once again, to stand with me as I journey to Little Rock, Arkansas, for a fateful confrontation with the button-down, pageboy Yale Law forces of the New Covenant.

To wit: On Thursday, I will fly into Little Rock on the Rolling Stone Gulf Stream 4—with Jann, Bill Grieder and P. J. O'Rourke—for a lengthy, cross-exam-style summit conference with Governor Clinton, Senator Gore and whichever of their ranking wizards might want to talk to us about questions and issues that I am just now putting together. It will be an extensive gig—probably 50 or 60 hours, but not all at once.

We will not inhale, under any circumstances. But that will not prevent us from grappling with bedrock issues. The agenda is wide open for now, and I figure that I/we might as well set at least a part of it.... We are, after all, the good guys. And if they're not, we may as well know it now, for good or ill.

So, what I need from you quickly—in addition to the cruel and heartless list of questions and National Association of Criminal Defense Lawyers position papers that I got today from Keith—is one question, in 20 words or less, that you would want to ask Bill Clinton if he promised to answer it and it was the only question he had time for.... Hell, Nancy, it could be anything at all. Just as long as it's quick and he can't hide from it.

There will by no shortage of questions. We are a profoundly eclectic task force. P. J. will fight to the death for Bush and Quayle. Grieder abandoned all hope when Tsongas went down. And Jann has his own agenda, which he feverishly keeps to himself....

So that leaves me. And I am, as you know, of the old school—the sacred Edward Bennett Williams ethic of massive retaliation.

That is my wa, Nancy. And I learned it from Ed, who was no stranger to drink or even craziness, on occasion. He was a monster, but so what? Ed was a warrior, and I loved him for it. If he was a monster, he was our monster, and on some days he walked point for all of us.... Remember what Joe Louis said when "he appeared out of nowhere"—as Ed put it—in that dim Seattle courtroom as a final character witness for Dave Beck and James Hoffa: "You can run but you can't hide."

That's how I want Bill Clinton to feel when we discuss the Fourth Amendment in Little Rock this weekend. And that's why I beseech you as a fellow director and warrior to send me one hardball question that will help me to deal effectively with the Clinton/Gore axis.

I am a smart boy, Nancy, but I am easily led astray and seduced into slick gibberish. So, yes. I need help now, and I ask no more of you than I do of all these other lazy bastards on our board.

The fox has been in our henhouse for many years, but now the coon is coming. And where the fuck is Big Ed? Now that I finally need him?

Indeed. The fat is in the fire, Nancy. The hog is out of the tunnel. If you believe in God, you must believe that He has chosen me to speak for us at this point in our tortured history....

As Ben Franklin said, "We must all hang together, or surely we will all hang separately."

Call me at any hour. For the first time in many moons, I will be registered at the Capital Hotel in Little Rock under my own name.

I am innocent, Nancy, and so are you. And so we pray is Bill Clinton.

—HST

Wed	**05 Aug 92**	*Washington Post* poll shows Bush's approval rating at 33 percent low
Wed	**05 Aug 92**	U.S. indicts four officers in Rodney King beating

Down + Out in Little Rock

the huge olympic-size banner at the entrance to Little Rock's Airport is taller than the AVIS building + about as long as a normal football field...

It was a hot
afternoon in Arkansas
as we approached
the Little Rock
Airport in a
long white Cadillac
Limosine with the
the sunroof open
& the TV set on
& iced whiskey drinks
Rattling in the
cheap go-cups
that we'd stolen
from Does downtown Cafe
where we'd just

had a nasty
little lunch with
Billy Clinton, the
Reigning Gov. of
Arkansas &
current odds-on
betting favorite to be
the next
President of The
United States.
I was not
especially happy to
be there and
neither was P.J.
O'Rourke ... mx

famous long-time
Fellow Traveler,
P.J. O'Rourke,
whose heart was
full of hate once
But not so
full as mine....
As we approached
the seedy little
entrance to what the sign said
was the "R.R. Apt," I
noticed another
genuinely HUGE
sign, at least as
long as a normal

football field—
that card =
Little Rock is →
→ Bush Country
ck this – maybe
Arkansas is etc.
Bush Ctry ???

"Jesus Christ,
that's horrible"

I said to nobody
in particular.

FORGET THE SHRIMP HONEY
I'M COMING HOME WITH THE CRABS

MEMO FROM THE NATIONAL AFFAIRS DESK: No. BB00086

(as in—Big Bill took three strikes and was 86'd...)

DATE: August 4, 1992

FROM: Dr. H. S. "No-Brainer" Thompson

SUBJECT: Mr. Bill's Neighborhood and who will live there...

HEADLINE: The Four Stooges meet Mr. Bill: Fear and loathing in Little Rock, tall gibberish at Doe's Café... What language do they speak at the Bank of Bangladesh?... And where were you when the fun stopped?...

Well, Bubba—you'll want to mix yourself a real stiff drink before you sit down to read this one, because it ain't gonna make you feel comfortable. No, I suspect it will make you feel queasy—just like it does me.

But so what? We are in the politics business, eh? And it is never calm or comfortable. No sooner do you run the fox out of the henhouse than the goddamn coon comes in, and that's what's happening now.... Sorry, Bubba, but I know you want me to tell you the truth.

I have just returned from a top-secret issues conference in Little Rock with our high-riding candidate, Bill Clinton—who is also the five-term governor of Arkansas and the only living depositor in the Bank of Bangladesh who wears a Rolling Stone T-shirt when he jogs past the hedges at sundown.

(Ah yes, the hedges. How little is known of them, eh? And I suspect, in fact, that the truth will never be known.... I wanted to check them out, but it didn't work. My rented Chrysler convertible turned into a kind of Trojan horse in reverse—and frankly, I was deeply afraid to stay for even one night in Little Rock by myself for fear of being tracked and seized and perhaps even jailed and humiliated, on instructions from nameless factotums at Clinton for President headquarters.)

It was ugly. We were under intense surveillance the whole time, despite our desperate efforts to act like just another gang of good ole boys for Clinton.

It was shameful. Clinton already had Jann Wenner's endorsement and the cover of Rolling Stone, so anything he said to us—me and P. J. O'Rourke and Dollar Bill Greider—was pretty much a matter of filigree. We were dupes.

We knew it would be eerie, but we did it anyway. And if it proved nothing at all, at least we weren't busted. Which is a very real danger these days—especially in Mr. Bill's Neighborhood, where the streets will be full of police.

There was no shortage of police to greet us when we arrived at the stately Capital Hotel in what appeared to be downtown Little Rock. As we pulled up to the entrance at about six in the evening, I looked out through the smoke-silver windows of the limo and saw to my horror that the whole sidewalk and even the lobby were alive with burly, angry-looking Secret Service agents with wires in their ears and an ominous curiosity about us.

"Ye fucking gods!" I said to Greider. "Look at those brutes! Are they waiting for us?" They were an ugly-looking lot, clearly the dregs of the SS presidential detail, and they eyed us with an unnatural hostility....

I am no stranger to the Secret Service. We have worked together for many years, with many candidates and often in very close quarters. And sometimes under very bizarre circumstances. But we long ago made a separate peace. They know me now, and we get along fine.

But something was wrong.

"This is your fault, goddamnit!" said P.J. "I'm going to end up in some goddamn Arkansas prison just for being seen with you. We're doomed. I knew I shouldn't have come on this stupid, evil trip."

"Nonsense," I said. "The governor must be inside waiting to greet us."

"Forget it," said the limo driver. "Marilyn Quayle is in town. These people are all big-time Republicans. They don't even know who you are."

"Wonderful," I said. "Probably we should make contact with Marilyn Quayle immediately. I want to get <u>her</u> side of the story."

"Bullshit!" said Greider. "Get me a wheelchair or I'll turn you in for uttering threats on her life."

"You swine," I said. "I'll put you out in the street and make you hitchhike down to the emergency room at St. Vincent's."

We had flown down to Little Rock in high style, lounging around on a jet plane the size of a Greyhound bus with only six seats, two telephones and gold-plated fixtures in a bathroom larger than some of the editorial offices at <u>Rolling Stone</u>.

We were the strike force, the Gang of Four, the eminent <u>Rolling Stone</u> blue-ribbon presidential forum—zooming into Little Rock at 600 miles an hour to confront the Democratic presidential candidate, Bill Clinton, and see who he really was.

Well... that didn't happen, for reasons that we will get to later. It was T. S. Eliot, I think, who wrote (in "The Hollow Men") "... Between the idea/And the reality... /Falls the Shadow." I was the shadow.

Bill Clinton was not comfortable being in the same room with me—presumably for image reasons—but he handled it pretty well. He is, after all, a career politician only 90 days away from the presidency—provided that he makes no mistakes between now and Election Day—and being involved in some kind of fracas in the back room of a downtown bar and grill with an "alleged" world-class dope fiend, drunkard and gun freak would definitely be a mistake.

Ah, but we are getting ahead of our story here.

Let's go back about 22 hours to our commando-like drop into the Little Rock airport—where a huge blue-and-white sign, bigger than <u>two</u> Greyhound buses, said: LITTLE ROCK IS BUSH COUNTRY.

"Jesus Christ," I muttered to P.J. "What are we doing here?"

"Speak for yourself," he said. "I feel right at home."

"Of course," I said. "You Nazi swine."

He grinned and ate another Percodan, to calm the pain in his gums.

"Do you have any more of those?" I asked him. "My broken back is killing me."

"No," he said. "I gave them all to Greider. I couldn't stand his pitiful screams any longer."

We were all injured. The plane was like a Civil War hospital. Greider, our éminence grise, had ripped all the tendons out of his knee in a freak accident only two hours earlier on the tarmac at the Teterboro, New Jersey, airport and was in extreme pain.

"Don't worry, Bubba," I said to him. "I'm a doctor. Here, eat these pills." I gave him 16 Advils, which he resisted but finally swallowed.

"I can't stand pain," I said. "Not even to be around it."

"Thank God you're here, Doc," he said. "We're all in this thing together."

That elegant dictum, a testament to brotherhood under stress, would be severely tested in the next 22 hours.... It was one nightmare after another, as we were plunged into Mr. Bill's Neighborhood, for good or ill.

THINNING OUT THE GENE POOL

Thomas Jefferson moves West, along with his brain-damaged brother...Little Rock is Bush Country, ho, ho...

WELCOME TO Arkansas. It is not much different from Brazil, when you get right down to it: just another gang of wild boys wanting to gouge a living out of the land. It is one of those free-fall kind of states—like Kentucky and Tennessee and Missouri—that was originally populated by drifters, fugitives, outlaws, gamblers and malcontents who mainly lived in the hills or worked the rivers, because it was hard to feel free in the flatlands where "civilization" flourished....

The Wild West wasn't always just beyond the Mississippi or the Rockies or the desperate, crazy cannibalism of Donner Pass.... It took three generations of high-rolling Americans to discover that St. Louis wasn't necessarily the western edge of the nation. We bought the whole Louisiana Purchase—16 states—from France for something like three cents an acre, and Jefferson was condemned as a spendthrift maniac for wasting that kind of money.

It was not long, however, before a tidal wave of dehumanized white trash swarmed into these territories and set up a whole hellbroth of "shops" that sold everything from snake oil and whiskey and Winchesters to white slaves and gambling and Jesus and bogus gold mines "just over the next range" of mountains....

A thriving trade grew up around the selling of "previously unavailable" seats on the next wooden-wheeled stagecoach to Denver, where the streets were paved with gold. And it was only a few days into the sunset, not far at all....

WELL...IT'S a long story, and we don't have time for it now. No. Our job now is to have a quick look at a long political tradition for Kentucky, Tennessee and Arkansas. Some of the best people—and a lot of the worst—have emerged from these hills and rich bottomlands as senators, governors, statesmen and famous political leaders. The line runs from Henry Clay and Andrew Jackson to the legendary William Fulbright of Arkansas and Albert Gore, Sr., of Tennessee.

They were the real thing. They gave politics a good name, win or lose. People who got up on Election Day to vote for Fulbright or Al, Sr., still talk about it with a sense of pride and even privilege to have voted for men who spoke to the better side of their natures and stood for what was right.

That is a very rare feeling these days, and the bedrock boosters of George Bush and Dan Quayle will never know it—which is sad, because it is a very elegant feeling to wake up in the morning and go down to your neighborhood polling place and come away feeling proud of the way you voted.

Take my word for it. I have been there, and it's *fun*....Even now, more than 30 years later, I still judge people on the basis of whether they voted for Jack Kennedy in 1960, or for Richard Nixon....Those bastards are scarred forever, and I'm not. At least not for that. Hell, it was an honor to be able to vote against Richard Nixon—and it will be an honor on November 3 to vote against George Bush and everything he stands for.

BILL CLINTON is very enthusiastic about the Grameen Bank of Bangladesh and everything it stands for.... Which is probably a good thing—at least Dollar Bill says it's good, and I have always trusted Greider's instincts, which are wise and shrewd and decent.... But Bill Clinton is also very enthusiastic about *law enforcement* and more *police* and re-hab *prisons* and the right of the U.S. military or paramilitary SWAT teams to pursue, destroy or kidnap *alleged* criminals in foreign countries, anywhere in the world.

Which bothers me—maybe in the same way that Clinton's being a Democrat bothers P.J. He is a Republican and I'm a criminal—if only because I have smoked, handled and frequently even enjoyed marijuana from time to time, and I see no reason to be rehabilitated or cured of that taste, just because a gang of faddish yahoos say marijuana is evil....

I know better, and so does Bill Clinton—along with Al and Tipper and steely-eyed little Hillary—but I am not running for president this year, and if I were I might tell Larry King that I "didn't inhale" the stuff either.

But I would say it with a smile, and would expect my friends to understand and smile with me. Why not? The yahoos *are* out there, and they are after us.

Ah, but the rub. Cazart! Yes. I see it all very clearly now. I was blind as a bat, but no longer.... So let me share it with you, Bubba: the fruits of my hard-earned wisdom. Stand back! Here is the terrible nut of it: **Bill Clinton has no sense of humor.**

And he eats a lot of French fries and laughs at the wrong times and often manifests clinical symptoms of schizophrenia. But he knows a good deal when he sees one, and on that murky Friday morning in Little Rock, *we* were the good deal he was looking at—the Four Stooges, direct from New York, flown in to legitimize the deal. It is eerie to think now that George Bush might have a better sense of humor than Bill Clinton.

But don't get me wrong, Bubba. We had fun, despite our various crippling injuries and my own humiliation when Clinton denounced every thought I uttered and every question I asked, as if I were criminally insane.... Which is rude, if nothing else, and I tend to take rudeness personally.

The encounter took place in the back room of an artificially degraded replica of a standard-brand Southern diner called "Doe's Eat Place" (which I will hereafter and previously refer to as Doe's Café because I like "Café" and I can't stand the cuteness of the other. . . . So bear with me, Bubba: This is a very painful story for me to tell).

The *encounter* was what we had come for, the *mano a mano* gig with the man we all agreed would probably be the next president of the United States—unless he fucks up between now and November 3. Which is possible. Remember Willie Horton. Remember Gary Hart. . . . Indeed. There are many rooms in the mansion, and there will always be wreckage in the fast lane. This is the nineties, Bubba, and there is no such thing as paranoia. It's all true.

Separated at birth? Dr. Thompson (left) *and Professor Carville*

So it is probably not fair to dismiss Bill Clinton as a cowardly, craven fool for feeling a touch apprehensive when his hare-brained scheduler set him up for an unprecedented and utterly unpredictable lunch forum of some kind with "The Editors of *Rolling Stone*," who were famous for savaging politicians.... It was a high-risk venture, for sure, and I had to like him for doing it.

IT IS hard to know exactly what the cover of *Rolling Stone* is worth to a front-running presidential candidate—but there is no question at all about the shit-rain of ugliness that could happen if the luncheon got out of hand. These drunken, brain-damaged brutes might do almost anything.

Which is a nice kind of reputation to have, in some towns—but not in Little Rock, when you're meeting in public with the next president in full view of the national press and 14 Secret Service watchdogs. Nobody needs a headline like: CLINTON INJURED IN WILD BRAWL WITH DOPE FIENDS: CANDIDATE DENIES DRUNKENNESS, CANCELS BUS TRIP, FLEES.

Worse things have happened, Bubba, and they usually come with no warning and for no good reason at all. A mad dog might come out of nowhere and sink its fangs into the flesh above your knee, then bite you repeatedly in the stomach. Certain death. Foaming at the mouth. Horrible. Horrible.

I was seized with this vision about three minutes after we sat down for a lunch of tamales, tuna fish and French fries with the next president, who was not real eager to be there. He behaved in a queer, distracted manner, and crushed my knuckles together when we shook hands. I shouted with pain, and Jann quickly intervened, saying, "Calm down, Governor. We're on *your* side."

I nodded meekly and sat down in a tin chair at what was either the head or the foot of the table—thinking that the candidate would naturally sit at the other end, far out of reach of me.

But *no*. The creepy bastard quickly sat down *right next to me*, about two feet away, and fixed me with a sleepy-looking stare that made me feel uneasy. His eyes narrowed to slits, and at first I thought he was dozing off....But he appeared to be very alert, very tense, as if he were ready to pounce.

Ye gods, I thought. What's *happening* here? This is not what I had in mind. The interview had turned weird, and so had the governor....Nobody else seemed to notice that I was paralyzed with fear.

But I was not totally brain-dead, and just as I felt myself on the brink of passing out, I remembered that I had a gift for Governor Clinton, who continued to stare at me darkly.

I reached quickly into my rumpled shirt pocket and pulled out a brand-new Vandoren tenor saxophone reed, which had been entrusted to me by the famous photographer "Fulton of Aspen," who also plays the tenor sax and had caught Clinton's act on the *Arsenio Hall Show*. "He sounds a little screechy," Fulton had told me. "He needs a pure Vandoren reed for that Selmer Mark VI he plays. Anything else sounds *cheap* in a Mark VI."

I got the governor's attention by gently waving the elegant little piece of bamboo back and forth in front of his eyes until he came vaguely alive and smiled at me....Hot damn, I thought. That was *close*. He seemed almost friendly now. I explained that the reed was a gift from a fellow musician who wished him well, then I pressed it into his outstretched palm.

The SS boys reacted like Dobermans when I made uninvited physical contact with the candidate and then gave him a small, unidentifiable object to put in his mouth. But I waved them off with a friendly smile. "Relax, boys," I said. "It's only a harmless reed—a tribute to the governor's *art*."

What happened next was so strange that I would have shrugged it off as one of those random, paranoid hallucinations that occur now and then, even to sane people—except that I have the whole long moment on Sony Hi8 Metal-E60 videotape, and there were also five or six witnesses who later recalled the incident with stark clarity and a creepy sense of dismay that none of them wanted to talk about or even acknowledge at the time. But it was true.

Clinton lifted the small Carlyle Hotel envelope toward his face and stared balefully at the reed for what seemed like a very long time, like a chimp peering into his mirror....There was a sense of puzzlement on his face as he silently pondered the thing.

It was an awkward moment, Bubba. *Very* awkward. Nobody knew how to handle it. He seemed unhappy, almost angry—as he fondled the reed distractedly and rolled it around in his fingers, saying nothing. . . . Then he rolled his eyes back in his head and uttered a wild quavering cry that made my blood run cold.

The others tried to pretend that it wasn't happening. We were, after all, in the South—and in some tangled way we were also the governor's *guests*. Or maybe he was *ours*. Who knows? Hill people are strange about manners. But there was no doubt that *somebody* was drifting over the line into unacceptable rudeness, and I didn't think it was *me*.

Then the governor dropped the reed on the table like it was just another half-eaten potato scrap, brushing it blankly aside and smiling warmly at all of us—as if he had just emerged from a pod and was happy to be among friends. "No more music," he said firmly. "Let's have some food, I'm *hungry*." Then he grasped the wicker basket of French fries with both hands and buried his face in it, making soft snorting sounds as he rooted around in the basket, trying vainly to finish it off.

I was afraid, but Jann was quick to recover. "Easy, Governor, easy," he said in a very suave voice. "Let me help you with that, Bill. Hell, we're *all* hungry." He smiled and reached out for the half-empty basket of French fries, as if to share the burden—but Clinton snatched it away, clutching it to his chest and saying nothing. . . .

Well, I thought. It can't get any weirder than this without all of us going to jail—so why not relax and act normal? Or at least try. These things happen. Buy the ticket, take the ride. Welcome to Mr. Bill's Neighborhood.

I CAME AWAY from Little Rock with mixed feelings. Bill Clinton and I did not hit it off real well, but so what? I got into politics a long time ago and I still believe, on some days, that it can be an honorable trade.... That is not an easy belief to hang on to after wallowing for 30 years in the belly of a beast that has beaten and broken more good men and women than crack and junk bonds combined. Politics is a mean business, and when September rolls around in a presidential campaign, it gets mean on a level that is beyond most people's comprehension. The White House is the most powerful office in the world, and a lot of people will tell you that *nothing* is over the line when it finally comes down to winning or losing the presidency of the United States. Nobody is safe and nothing is sacred when the stakes finally get that high. It is the ultimate fast lane, and the people still on their feet in September are usually the meanest of the mean. The last train out of any station will not be full of nice guys.

Look at George Bush. He is a monster and a fraud and a failure, and he has worked overtime to give politics a bad name. He is a mean-spirited wimp and a career bureaucrat who has arguably committed more high crimes and misdemeanors in and around the Oval Office than Richard Nixon would have been impeached for if he hadn't resigned.... Nixon was genetically dishonest and so is Bush. They both represent what Bobby Kennedy called "the dark underbelly of the American dream."

And Bill Clinton does not. Clinton is a decent man and a credit to his race. Ho, ho. That's a *joke*, Bubba. George Bush wouldn't laugh at it and neither did Mr. Bill when I shook his hand and said it to him with a nice smile. He gave me another one of those weird sleepy-eyed stares and wished me good luck for the rest of my life.

Tue	**11 Aug 92**	Bush denies reports of affair in 1984 with aide
Tue	**11 Aug 92**	GOP votes platform calling for constitutional amendment outlawing abortion

LET'S FACE it, Bubba. The main reason I'll vote for Bill Clinton is George Bush, and it has been that way from the start.... There is no way around it (for me) and no reason to apologize for it. George Bush is a dangerously failed president and a half-bright top-level nerd who has spent the last four years avoiding grocery stores and gas stations while he tried to keep tabs on the disastrous fallout from the orgy of greed and short-selling that was the "Reagan Revolution."

He has dutifully presided over what he and his people have believed all along is the end of the American century—the inevitable collapse of an impossible democracy brought low by niggers, unions and dope fiends. He has no more real faith in the future of America than he does in the future of Iraq, and in his heart he is not especially eager to do another four years in the Big House and go down in history as another Herbert Hoover.... It is not out of line in the White House, these days, to suggest in whatever passes for privacy that George might be better off *losing* a professionally tainted election and let the economy collapse on Bill Clinton instead of the GOP.

Many career Democrats feel the same way. It was not some queer shift of the jet stream that caused Bill Bradley, Sam Nunn, Dick Gephardt and Mario Cuomo to lay low in '92.... No. It was an educated fear of the coming shit-rain and a "gut instinct" of their own highly paid advisors, who said it might be "a lot smarter" to wait and make their move in 1996. Which may be true. Calvin Coolidge had the same instinct in the summer of '28, when he ducked out and ran like a rat.

Which reminds me, Clinton's appeal is obviously relative. Leaving Little Rock was a narrow escape...so be warned: Your ACLU card won't get you anything but a *beating* at Clinton headquarters. Albert Speer would have recognized these people in his dreams.

Q—*What happened to Hitler's dream of breeding a race of super Aryan youth?*

A—Come on down to Little Rock, Bubba. See you at Doe's Café—just around the corner from Clinton headquarters.

And I guess it was Jann who said that "Clinton is like a cross between Dan Quayle and Calvin Coolidge."

Well. . . shucks, Bubba. Maybe it was *me* who said that.

Congress of the United States
House of Representatives
Washington, D.C. 20515

8/10/92
To: Jann

Okay. I am now going back to the drawing board to come up with a better and more valid reason to vote for Clinton in November—which I plan to do, but my reasons are no more concrete today than they were on the flight down to Little Rock. I like him a little better, but there was nothing in what he said for the record to excite anybody except cops, money-mongers and elitist policy wonks. The rest is all a matter of blind faith and reading between the lines.

Taken at face value, Clinton's stated agenda is a benign, neohumane mix of Paul Tsongas, Ross Perot and the ghost of Jimmy Carter—along with touches of John Kennedy, Franklin Roosevelt, and Ronald Reagan in a generous mood. There is no reason, on the evidence, to believe that a Clinton administration will be anything but a grim, four-year struggle with bad debts, bankruptcies and crisis economics. And nothing he told us in Little Rock was either personally or politically reassuring to me vis-à-vis peace, prosperity and personal freedom from harassment, in our own private lives, by a new wave of tax-funded money-quacks, social workers and a bizarre task force of zealous, amateur cops with personal axes to grind.

Well, I thought. Win some, lose some. Maybe Hillary will get a whoop out of it—and I knew James Carville would, for sure.

No assessment of Clinton or the pros and cons of a guaranteed volatile Clinton presidency would be accurate if it didn't include the Carville factor.... James is a wild boy, they say—a mean joke on wheels who grows new teeth just as fast as he breaks them off in the flesh of the enemy. He is a professional warrior, maybe the fastest and meanest hired gun in the politics business this year, and James is a barrel of laughs.

OUR VOTE ON the flight down to Little Rock was three-to-one for Clinton, and it was still three-to-one on the flight back to New York. Nobody had changed their mind about how to vote in November, despite a few radical shifts of attitude.

Jann had been very jittery on Thursday, and Dollar Bill was gloomy. Jann feared the unknown, and Greider was afraid we might be walking into an ambush, that Clinton was such a pure politician that he might use us for some kind of treacherous publicity stunt—like denouncing us in public and holding us up for ridicule by the national press, as "a perfect example of the kind of Judas goats that I don't want to endorse me in this election."

"Don't kid yourself," he warned me. "This guy is a pure politician. He has no conscience at all. He would trash us in public and denounce us as traitors if he thought it would boost him five points in the polls."

"They all would," I said. "They would burn us at the stake on network TV if they thought it would put them in the White House."

8/10/92
To: Jann

Okay. We still have a problem with my inability to explain why I feel very strongly about voting for Bill Clinton on November 3—except that four more years of the Reagan-Bush band will mean the death of hope and the loss of any sense of possibility in politics for a whole generation that desperately needs that fix and will wither on the vine without it.

That is reason enough to vote for Clinton. It helps that I like him as a person and trust him enough as a quality politician to believe that I can occasionally turn my back on him when he moves into the White House—which he will, I think, and I will help him in every way I can, short of guaranteeing in print that President Clinton/Gore will solve all our problems and give 40 acres and a mule to everybody who votes for him.

Nobody is going to do that.

So what the fuck? Let's kick those rat-bastards out of the temple and put one of our own people in charge. We have nothing to lose except fun and the joy of watching a serious brawler go to war with the greedheads. Why not? Rumble.

—HST

8/17
To: Myself

It is 4:27 A.M. on a gloomy Monday morning and I'm about to have a look at the news on TV.... Tupelo is the hot dateline this morning. Hot damn! It's Elvis Day. He was born in Tupelo.

And Madonna was born in Southfield, Michigan. That is another hot spot today. Or maybe it was yesterday. Shit, the news gets faster and faster. CNN is beginning to look like a retooled version of The History of the United States from Start to Finish in 199 Seconds.... It was a huge hit 20 years ago, especially when the heavily censored TV version was edited down to 90 seconds. The Civil War and the history of aviation needed only five seconds each.

Ye gods. Now it is Saddam Hussein, Bill Clinton and George Bush, all getting ready for war. Clinton is wistfully fondling a laughing little black girl, pressing her head against his thigh while he spoke to reporters about the firestorm of cheap, rotten, brainless, low-rent lies that he knows will erupt this week out of Houston, when Bush and his low-rent beaters will kick off their long-awaited avalanche of ugliness against everything he stands for or was ever even tempted to do.

George Bush sucking wind in public once again—bitterly denying a story in Saturday's New York Times that said U.S. fighter-bombers would launch a major air strike against Iraq on Monday morning, in order to boost the president's sagging position in the popularity polls by going back to war and whipping the voters into patriotic frenzy.... It was true, but he was forced to deny it repeatedly on national TV for something like 29 straight hours.

8/19/92

To: Jann

By the time you get this memo, half of Baghdad will be ashes. The first strike was originally set for noon on Monday (dot-zero Washington), to make the network evening news deadlines and the front page of <u>all</u> morning papers.... It was a stroke of genius, a surefire guaranteed master plan for putting Weird George back in the White House....

The strike is back on. For tomorrow. Noon EDT. Take my word for it: George Bush is half man and half ape. Or was that Mr. Bill? Shit. You never know, these days. They're all gash-hounds in New Hampshire, but California is a different story, eh?

You bet! It's a hard goddamn dollar, for sure, and I pray with all my strength that I will never go through it again. Jesus! New Hampshire is like Peter Pan and Wendy on the road. And California—only four months later—is like Caligula and the Five Dwarfs.... It is out of hand, by then, no matter which side you're on. Win or lose, the die is almost cast by the time you hit California. The glue has hardened and you are fixed in it—and the only thing left is election night.

Ye fucking gods! Election night. It is the final, hideous orgasm for any political campaign.... Nobody knows why, except me—

No. That's a lie. There are others. But not many. And most of them are gone now, for good or ill. Either dead or gone or murdered like Bobby Kennedy, who understood the wild energies of a big-time, fast-lane, kill-or-be-killed modern American political campaign better than anybody and might still be president today if Roosevelt Grier had been man enough to stand tall and take that dinky little .22 caliber bullet in his own chest instead of ducking aside and letting it hit Bobby in the brain.

That is one way to understand politics: Not wisely but too well, in a kind of retrospective sense—and Bobby Kennedy is still the only presidential candidate in American history to be gunned down and publicly murdered on election night, in the throes of his highest moment.

Hunter

Fri 21 Aug 92 Post-convention polls

	Washington Post		CNN	
	Bush	**37%**	Bush	39%
	Clinton	**46%**	Clinton	51%

Dr. Hunter S. Thompson: National Correspondent

To:

George the Greek
— Clinton Hq.

Don't let that evil bastard even *pretend* that he's closed the gap to single-digits.

Bill *must* do something *dynamic* immediately: He'd get a lot of good ink by offering to send Woody Allen to *sex-Rehab* at his own expense.

OR invite the star-crossed Dutchess of York to Little Rock to *Jog* with him on Rainy afternoons.

Okay. You're welcome.

Best,

H. ST

Hunter

Owl Farm, Woody Creek, Colorado 81656

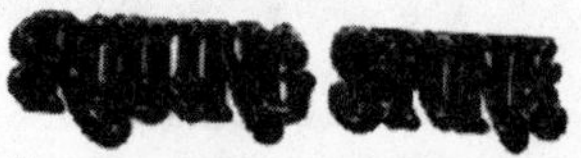

Dr. Hunter S. Thompson: National Correspondent

8/22

To: Ed Turner/CNN

Dear Ed...

You must be out of your fucking mind to believe that your Bush/Quayle albatross gained 17 points in the polls (in three days) because they soared like eagles out of the Houston convention. I am shocked by this horrible news-managed swill that I'm seeing on CNN <u>right now</u> (6:17 A.M. 8/22/92)—that George Bush is so much faster than Carl Lewis that he is suddenly (today) only two points behind Clinton, according to some alleged "popularity poll" by CBS and the <u>New York Times</u>.

Where did you get those numbers, Ed? From Mary Matalin?

And what the fuck is a "popularity poll," anyway? And why is Charles Bierbauer reporting from the White House that Bush was whipped into a frenzy of shrewd optimism when he got the news that he was "only 10 to 12 points behind in the polls"???

Whoops. Here is <u>Headline News</u> again, saying, "It looks like a dead heat."

Jesus! I'll tell you what it looks like to <u>me</u>, Ed: It looks like a classic case of whiskey journalism—like some rum-dumb geek on the midnight news desk ran amok when he got what he will swear forever was a "dead-serious top-security telephone call from the White House switchboard; yeah, it was a woman's voice, kind of sultry." Right. And the sultry voice asked him if he could "stand by for Mr. Baker?"

You bet, ma'am. Me and James go <u>way</u> back. Hell, I'm from Texas. I'm a newshound.

Owl Farm, Woody Creek, Colorado 81656

"*Hi*, fella. This is James Baker in the White House. You got a minute?"

"You bet, Senator. I'm all ears. How can I help you tonight? Can we put you on *live*?"

"Never in hell, son. You put me on live and you'll be dead as a doornail real quick. Just shut up and write these numbers down."

"Yes, *sir*. Of course. Yes. Please forgive me, sir. I was only kidding about putting you on 'live.' Hell *no*. We would *never* do that."

"Me either, son. I would *never* threaten to have a man butchered in his own bathtub for revealing the source of confidential top-secret White House information. I could *do* that, but it would be wrong—wouldn't it?"

"*Absolutely*, sir! *Totally* wrong...But you don't have to worry about *me*, sir. This call never happened. We never spoke. Just like Deep Throat."

"Exactly, son. Exactly. I knew I could trust you: We had you checked out. [Pause.] But you *will* need these numbers, right? Yes. You *will*—unless you want to spend the next 10 years of your life in a federal prison for perjury. [Shrieks of dopey laughter in background; "Baker's" voice fades in and out, then barks angrily.] Shut up! Get a pencil. Here it is. You got yourself a scoop. Stop whining and *listen*.... Bush is 46 percent and rising. Clinton is 48 percent and sinking like a stone. I just got the secret advance figures, son, and I'm truly amazed. The president has been gaining about one point *every hour*. By morning he will be *ahead*. It's amazing! I've scheduled a press conference at sundown, when the president will call for Bill Clinton to drop out of the race."

"What? Drop out?"

"You heard me, fella. And you better write it just like I said it. Remember. We know where you live. We monitor your bank account and we have keys to every lock in your house. [Wild hoots of laughter in background as "Baker" signs off.] So long for now, son. Just remember what I told you: dead heat, amazing Bush turnaround stuns Clinton as millions rally to cheer commander in chief—Demos panic as lead shrinks, Clinton helpless, General Baker seizes reins as U.S. jets strike Baghdad—Bush triumphant in Gulfport, asks Army for support as Barbara mocks Hillary. Okay, got it, boy?"

"Yes, sir: 46 up, 48 down, Clinton doomed. Bush rallies, dead heat. Only two points, no hope, fat lady sings, Arkys demoralized, General Baker says, 'We will march on a road of bones.'"

"Good work, fella—except for that stuff about bones. I didn't say that, son. George Bush said it. But you can't quote him, remember? Or me either, goddamnit. That was our deal."

"You bet, sir. The fat lady said it. Trust me. I'm smart."

"Of course you are, son. Otherwise you might be dead. Or <u>chopped up</u> someplace, like Hoffa."

"I didn't hear that, sir. It sounded like a radio up the street."

"What you heard, son, was the fat lady. She was singing."

"Yes, sir. But not for <u>me</u>. Please!"

"No, Bubba. Not yet. Not as long as you're an asset."

Well...shucks, Ed. But never mind. I can't continue. <u>Being There</u> has appeared on my gigantic TV screen—so I guess it's all over for you and me and my questions about possible White House intimidation (or worse) at CNN and the dread specter of a poll-rigging scandal.

No, Ed—that would be wrong. I will not abandon you now, just because of some sot on the night desk, and I always feel better just to be in the same room with Chauncey Gardiner. He's funny and you're not—at least not today, while you're still peddling this crooked whore-faced gibberish about Bush closing the gap to two points without even breaking a sweat.

Loose lips sink ships, Ed. And if Bush gets another four years, even <u>you</u> might be put in prison.... Think about it. We can make a

deal: If you're right, I will shave my head as a feature on your Oriental news hour—and if you're wrong, you will shave your head on Crossfire.... On Monday. Yes. We are too short on time to start whooping it up by spreading kinky rumors about popularity polls. I have a date in Little Rock on the night of November 3, Ed, and I don't want it to turn weird on me—and especially not because of something you did.

It would be awkward, Ed, and we don't need it. Why should we

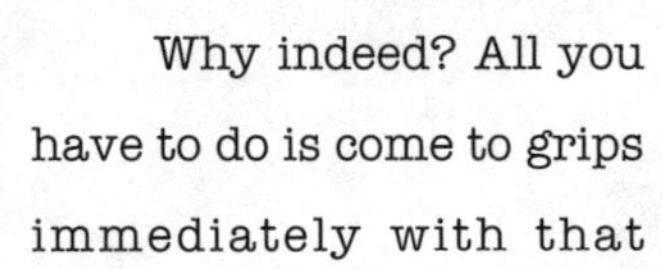

turn into savage hyenas?

Why indeed? All you have to do is come to grips immediately with that

sold-out screwhead botch that was running every goddamn 30 minutes on Headline until I switched over to Being There.

I hope to God it won't be there when I switch back to your "news," Ed. I probably couldn't stand it.... I just got back from Little Rock, in fact, where I had a bizarre confrontation with Mr. Bill on his own turf. He said I should be in prison, and then he laughed like a loon and offered me a bunch of French fries that he'd crushed and squeezed in his hands. It was horrible.

What the hell? ... Progress marches on, eh? My grandmother was the first president of GE and my grandfather was Korean.... So now is the time to act, Ed. Do it now. Do it for us. Sober up and get a grip on your news organization. They need leadership—not brainless jabbering in the darkness, like you hear on some nights in Little Rock.

But so what? Stand tall, Ed. The time has come. Take my word for it. I understand these things.

Good luck,

Doc

8/24

Dear Doc:

Your satellite dishes got skewed by some case of empties tossed from a passing school bus out there. That was the White House Channel (between the Lost Luggage Channel and the Restroom Channel) that you were watching, and those were not polling numbers; that's D.C. code for numbers of hapless print reporters slaughtered like Bosnians by the powers who really run things, and no one really cares very much because they don't work in television and thus have the worth of a Lebanese pound note.

As to the phone call you copied—accurately, I am pleased to note—it is vital to know that it was from Jim Baker, but not the Jim Baker lately of the State Department. It was from the Jim Baker lately of Tammy Fay fame and the alert deskie simply played along with the poor loon as he worked out his fantasy, not unlike editors of an aging magazine that once claimed to play the internal organs of the teenie readers, much as the ghost of Marilyn the M spooks the elders of this country. Bill Clinton is dating her ghost by the way, a story we are working on, with pictures of him alone (since ghosts don't photograph) that prove our thesis, one paid for and approved by the White House and which will guarantee me appointment to the Court of St. James, a small motel on the outskirts of Atlanta, and I will go anywhere skirts are to...

And, just so you will understand for historical purposes, there was no convention in Houston. What you saw was a videotape produced by the GOP and given to all networks for playback during last week. It saves us jillions of dollars and permits us to attend our

Bathist training camps as we prepare for Saddam's takeover. You haven't heard him compared to Hitler lately, have you? And now you know why. And it made my former staffer Pat Buchanan uneasy, since he is still digging around in Bittburg at their old cemetery, where he forced the poor old Gipper to go one cold winter day a few years ago, causing his hair to turn bright red overnight. I was standing in our anchor booth one night in Houston with Novak and Sununu, and Novak was irritated over the cross-dressing of journalists as government employees and said, "In all my 35 years in Washington, I have never been offered a job in government or politics," and Sununu reflected briefly and said, "Well, Novak, there is a reason for that, of course. Work in government or politics requires at least a bare minimum of qualifications." Novak was not amused, but I was (I amuse easily, as you can tell). It seemed odd that Jerry Brown did not turn up, given the number of TV cameras in Houston. Like a moth to a burning hospital is old Jerry. Your friend Jesse is still angry, by the way. Don't look for him much down among the flowering Bubbas who are tortured with their Yale/Oxford/St. Albans accents and wives who could take Maggie Thatcher at question time in Commons at the drop of a grit. Yep, Doc, there is a conspiracy, but it is so cleverly hidden you haven't found it, because you have not looked in the right place: a safe house near Little Rock is all I can tell you now. Watch CNN. We are the world's most important something.

ET

NEW POLICY MEMO FROM THE NATIONAL AFFAIRS DESK
#009XXX1

To: All Rolling Stone Staff & Security Personnel

From: RAOUL DUKE, Sports

Date: August 24, 1992

Subject: EMERGENCY PROCEDURES in re PATRICK BUCHANAN and your PERSONAL DANGER...Beware of Attacks or Violent Invasions of Our Office Area...Journalism is a Brutal Business

All repeat All R.S. staff, editors & employees are warned as of today (8/24/92) that neither George Bush nor Patrick Buchanan shall be allowed to enter any Rolling Stone office for any reason until further notice.

Nor shall any person in the pay of any FEDERAL POLICE AGENCY be admitted to any R.S. office-area for any reason at any time of any day or night without a VALID Search or Arrest WARRANT.

Mon 24 Aug 92 Quayle calls Clinton "Slick Willie" again

Wed 26 Aug 92 A mistrial is declared in the case of CIA official Claire George, charged with lying to Congress about knowledge of the Iran-contra program

Wed 26 Aug 92 *New York Times* poll shows Clinton gain and Bush drop

Aug 24		Aug 20	
Bush	36%	Bush	42%
Clinton	51%	Clinton	45%

Aug 25-92

~~1290 Avenue of the Americas New York, NY 10104 (212)484-1616~~

D.C. OFFICE

TO HST:

HERE'S THE DEAL. GO OUT ON THE ROAD NEXT WEEK IN THE SERVICE OF YOUR COUNTRY. SPEND TWO-THREE DAYS WITH BUSH & THEN RIP HIS LUNGS OUT IN PAGES OF RS.

IF YOU ACCEPT THIS ASSIGNMENT, I WILL MAKE SURE THE NOBLE ERIC GOES WITH YOU. IT WOULD BE GOOD FOR HIS EDUCATION — WATCHING YOU WORK IN THE PRESENCE OF REAL DANGER!

SAY YES! YOUR PAL, THE GRAY EMINENCE

NO NO NO NO NO

(from Bill Greider)

To: Dollar Bill

GONZO

Aug 26 '92
Owl Farm

To: DB

You treacherous jabbering pimp! I have people in Washington who will jerk you up by the back of your pants and shoot you full of angel dust and slam you onto the Bush campaign bus with your nails painted pink and your mouth blazing fiery red lipstick and your fly open and the tips sliced off of your thumbs.

> **Yeah. "Here comes that babbling asshole from Rolling Stone again. What a horrible mess! He can't even talk. Did you see what those freaks wrote about the president? It's horrible. I can't stand the sight of Rolling Stone.... His name is Greider. Get him off the bus. Have him locked up. Scum like this gives honest journalism a black eye."**

Soon come, Bubba. Soon come...Shit. You're lower than a Judas goat. Why don't you call Fitzwater and tell him you want to hang out with George Bush for a few days? You know some bitching rock 'n' roll jokes. But what you really want to do is invite George to meet the Rolling Stone blue-ribbon forum next week in the back room of a nice biker S&M roadhouse on South Main Street in Houston called the Blue Fox. He'll know the place for sure, or at least his people will. Don't worry. Full bar, casual dress, come alone....

Good luck, Bubba. Sorry I can't be with you on this one, but I have to be in Louisville with my aged mother and address the Kentucky Literacy Foundation.

#2
August 26-92

RollingStone

1290 Avenue of the Americas New York NY 10104 (212) 484-1616

D.C. BUREAU

HST:

I RECEIVED YOUR FAX
& INTERESTING ATTACHMENTS.
IS THAT A "YES"?

NO

TIME IS SHORT. DON'T
MISS THE MOMENT.
CALL ME!

With warm regards, your friend,
Bill

Get back to work
+ stop this
whoring around
Good luck
Doc

CHAPTER 7

AUTUMN MADNESS

Whooping it up in London, Louisville and Paraguay...Secret vacation with the royal family...Haggling with Hillary, cruel warnings about Mr. Bill...Faxing frenzy with James and George and Jimmy and Big Ed on the need to destroy Ross Perot...

Tue	**01 Sep 92**	Clinton tells seniors Bush will cut Medicare			
Tue	**01 Sep 92**	Gore attacks Bush/Quayle re family values			
Wed	**02 Sep 92**	*New York Times* tracks *Washington Post* and ABC post-convention polls			
			ABC	*Washington Post*	ABC/*WP*
			Aug 21–23	Aug 21–25	Aug 26–30
		Bush	42%	41%	36%
		Clinton	47%	51%	55%
Mon	**07 Sep 92**	Baboon liver recipient dies			

AS SEPTEMBER rolled around I went into seclusion with my animals and began making plans to leave the country and move to Paraguay if George Bush got reelected. Some people called me paranoid, but *their* names were not on the U.S. Secret Service hot-list of known malcontents, addicts, drinkers and sworn political enemies with large weapons collections and erratic personal histories including (bogus) allegations of uttering public "threats" on the life of the president or vice president.

Both, in my case—but only because George Bush had been elected to both offices.

It was all nonsense, of course. I have been on good and mutually respectful terms with the Secret Service for 29 years and have been left alone for long periods of time with more presidents, candidates, senators, prime ministers and even foreign royalty than anybody since Bernard Baruch.

Well…shucks. That might be stretching it, but not much. The point is that the Secret Service stopped worrying about me a long time ago. Three generations of agents have been exposed to my sense of humor, and a few have become personal friends. I autograph my books for their children.

Wonderful, eh? But so what? I have friends in the White House, I have friends in prison, I have friends in Ecuador and New Orleans and Russia—and I communicate with all of them instantly, along with a lot of other people, by means of my fax equipment, just like I did with friends on the Corridor of Power on the third floor of Clinton's campaign headquarters in Little Rock and Ed Turner in Atlanta and George McGovern in Washington and my mother in Louisville and my son in Boulder and Ken Kesey in Oregon and Lynn Nesbit in New York and Earl Biss in Newport and Laila Nabulsi in Syria and John Walsh in Connecticut and Jack Nicholson in Los Angeles and Mike Stepanian in San Francisco and Terry in Moscow and Tom at the Jail and Ross Perot in Dallas and Ralph Steadman in England and Deborah in Utah and my friend The Professor in prison and Semmes in Clarksdale and Jimmy Buffet in Palm Beach and Jim Mitchell at the O'Farrell Theatre and Jennifer in Sacramento and Ed Bradley at CBS and Lyle Lovett in Texas and Dan Dibble in Albany and Jo Hudson in Big Sur and David Rosenthal at Random House and Catherine Conover in the place where they keep deaf people and George Stranahan up the road in Woody Creek and Doug Brinkley on the Magic Bus and William Burroughs in Kansas and Johnny Cusak in Pittsburgh…

I am a busy man on the fax machine.

It hums and beeps and spits paper at me 24 hours a day. Strange messages come hissing into my home from all over the world. The thing is never turned off. It provides a constant flow of hateful, brainless gibberish from people who dialed a wrong number and poured out their hearts and plans and crucial emergency orders for things like drone-generators and dildos that baffle my secretary and jam the laser drum with burning paper and screeching orange lights. I hate the fucking thing and I am always surprised when people actually respond to it.

Right. And so much for this useless, make-work bullshit. I am tired of explaining the Obvious. The following pages are clearly late-night, ill-advised facsimile messages sent to the people they are clearly addressed to, on the dates that are clearly marked, and anybody who can't understand it will never have read this far, anyway. So it's all moot. Do yourself a favor and skip the next few pages. Cut to the end. That's where the fun is. Take my word for it. By this time, you know all you want to know about Bill Clinton and James Carville and George Stephanopoulos. They are politicians, nothing more. The truth is not in them, and they like it that way. That is their job. And mine,tonight, is to quit typing this mean, redundant gibberish and get on to other things. Nevermind this filigree. If you're looking for the good parts, fan the pages until you see the word "Nixon." Nevermind Clinton. He is just a dip in the road. Selah.

Editor's note: *We interrupt the 1992 presidential race for a brief examination of that other great democracy, the United Kingdom. The nation where, you may recall, Bill Clinton didn't inhale...*

To: The Observer
From: HST

Dear Simon,

Okay. Rest easy. Fear nothing...

Stand back. My final analysis of the Royal Family Today is almost finished and will soon be oozing out of your fax, for good or ill.... In the fateful words of Lloyd George: "You rarely get what you need, but even a fool can get what he wants."

Or she. Indeed. We want to keep in mind that the British royal family is generally seen as a kind of bloodless pan-sexual tribe that is mainly well mannered and extremely well paid, but not much else. They are not even expected to be smart—much less wild and romantic and humorous.

That is not their main job. No. The main job of the royal family is politics, and they have done pretty well at it recently. They are business people, and they have a very shrewd understanding of their job description, which is brutal and extremely lucrative.

At a basic $170 or $180 million a year, tax-free, the queen of England is the highest-(legally)paid executive in the world, and the next king will be paid even better. There is huge money in being a royal. Even poor berserk Fergie earns four or five times as much as George Bush does as president of the United States.

Which is fair, I think—if only because Fergie has done her job better than George has done his. If Fergie and Diana were the daughters of President and Mrs. Bush, things would be very different today in the White House. Good old Barbara would be ordering new drapes for the East Wing and stylish new prayer rugs for the Lincoln Room, instead of preparing to pack up and flee.

If Fergie and Di were the Bush sisters, Bill Clinton would have been bumped off Page One about two years ago and poor, long-suffering Papa George would be running about 70 to 30 percent over any challenger in the polls today. With a pair of daughters like that, he might even be nominated for a third term. There is nothing like a flash of royal nipples on the front page to divert the public mind from a crashing, desperate economy: Never mind the rent, Bubba—just look at these jiggling tits.

It is no accident, Simon, that the behavior of the royal family deteriorates most horribly on days (weeks, months, etc.) when the level of sterling falls most horribly on the worldwide currency markets. God only knows what lewd and crazy acts the royals might be forced to commit if John Major ever even thought about devaluing the pound.

Which he has, of course—and so has Princess Diana, who clearly dreads it. But so what? So do I. And so will you, before this is over, because the price this time will be ghastly. "There are only so many orgies she can confess to," said one nervous tabloid journalist, "until finally she will lose all of her headline value and be tossed aside like a sail-cat."

What it looks like to me is a serious power struggle that will probably end very soon with either President Major or a 10-year-old child-king with a (relatively) nubile Queen Mother who is capable of causing serious trouble for many years if she doesn't get her way—and even if she does, for that matter, because a 31-year-old mother of the king who looks even vaguely like Sophia Loren is certain to rock many boats as she drifts from port to port like a wandering storm.

***Editor's note:** We now return you to the regularly scheduled Campaign '92.*

Tue	**15 Sep 92**	New planetary object detected beyond Pluto
Wed	**16 Sep 92**	***New York Times* poll shows:** **Bush 34 percent, Clinton 42 percent, Perot 14 percent**
Thu	**17 Sep 92**	Prosecutor ends Iran-contra inquiry
Fri	**18 Sep 92**	Perot petitions filed in last of 50 states

News—Urgent

Friday September 18 1992

Owl Farm

Campaign '92 Bulletin

ED TURNER: CNN

Ye fucking gods, Ed. You've squeezed your goddamn sound bytes down to an average 2.2 seconds and now you're letting Mason Williams and James Baker III take over your programming to claim that Bush has "closed the gap" from 23 points down to 9 points in 10 days by calling poor Mr. Bill a "draft-dodger."

You evil bastard. Where was Ronald Reagan in 1941–45? Probably on the Bataan March, eh?

HST

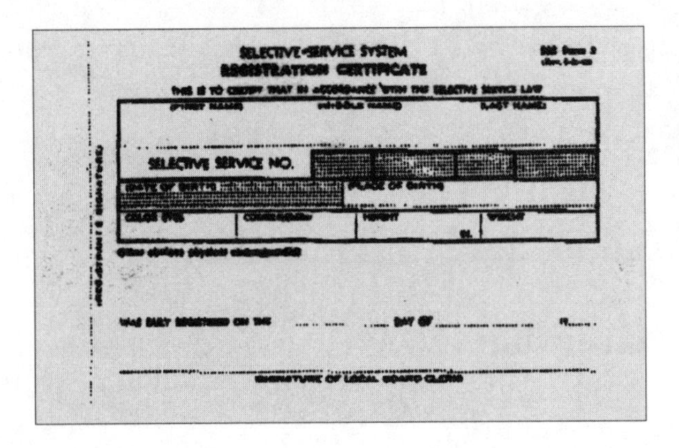

SELECTIVE SERVICE SYSTEM
REGISTRATION CERTIFICATE

SELECTIVE SERVICE NO.

Jann

Here is a nine-page memo I sent to James Carville, in re our (me and James's) long phone conversation earlier last night (Tuesday) about rumors (repeat, rumors) I picked up yesterday about a possible Bush/Baker strike on Iraq before the election—probably to take the head of Saddam Hussein.

That is extrapolation, of course, but the nut of it has to do with the whereabouts (now) and current destination(s) of the U.S.S. hospital ships Mercy and Comfort, which are possibly en route (now) from Oakland and Guam to the Persian Gulf for widely unknown reasons.

My "information" comes from a merchant seaman (here) who was suddenly ordered to quit his vacation and report at once to Alameda, California, and then fly to Guam to get aboard the Mercy and then to Iraq. Immediately (see details below, pages 1 to 3). If there is any truth at all in this rumor (which makes perfect political sense) then I have stumbled on a loose end (one of many) dangling off of a very big story. I have discussed it with James, Ed Turner, the Examiner, the sheriff, and a few other possible legman/sources/etc. We should have a far better fix on it by tonight—mainly the whereabouts of Prince Bandar and the hospital ships.

Read the bizarre pages (below); I like this story. It's fun. Okay,

H.

September 23, 1992

Owl Farm

James Carville

Clinton Headquarters

Little Rock, Arkansas

James:

Have you checked on the location(s) of the U.S.S. hospital ships Comfort and Mercy? My telephone tip of last night was definitely a straw in the wind and probably bullshit—but if there is anything to it, we should know at once. (If you find the Comfort and the Mercy in Guam, for instance—painted black and preparing to weigh anchor—let me respectfully suggest that you low-rent, backwoods, potato-sucking, hell-doomed carpetbaggers might want to pay some attention to it. There are not a lot of reasons why the U.S. would be sending two huge "battle-tested" hospital ships back to the Persian Gulf at this hardball point in time.)

Take my word for it, James—these lying, whorish swine will stop at nothing. How many points do you think Baker 3 believes it might be worth to Bush if he could strut out on the South Lawn of the White House on October 15 and display the still-bleeding head of Saddam Hussein on a silver platter?

Big points in Texas, James—and spontaneous riots of Bush fever all over Dade County. Hell, that head might be worth 10 points, nationwide. Think about it.

There is another small point of information on this, James, which has to do with my new neighbor: Prince Bandar of Saudi Arabia, brother of the king and Saudi Ambassador to the U.S.

Last Saturday (9/19), about 9 or 10 o'clock at night, the black sky over my home was rent by the thunderous noise of a low-flying U.S. military helicopter, en route to Bandar's house about a mile up the valley from mine (which is in Woody Creek, James, not in Aspen. There is a big difference, and Bandar is only on the cusp of it).

Bandar does not normally arrive in this fashion—and if he departed that way (other witnesses swear they saw/heard three military choppers), it was a blatant display of urgency. Bush would not move without Him "on board."

Ah...but so what, eh? There are many rooms in the mansion, James, and we will never be privy to all of them.

As for fleet movements—they're not essential in that every other ordnance (weapons, bombs, boats, etc.) except hospital ships is already in place over there...and they won't really need hospital ships, anyway.

Not to take Saddam's head...Shit, even a phoney head would look good for a South Lawn photo op on October 15. Who's going to call the president a liar when he's parading around in public with a rotting human head that he says is Saddam Hussein's?

Not me, James. And probably not you either. Because there will be a certain resemblance. And you know how those sand-niggers are about using body-doubles. Hell, they all look alike, anyway...and Baker 3 would bring some hideous quack to certify that the head was Saddam's for sure.

So beware, James, beware. Baker 3 is so mean that he makes you look like a garden snake. He would serve up the head of Barbara Bush on a platter if he thought it would win the election.

But I'm not telling you anything you don't already know, am I? Politics is a weird business, with many loose ends—

Which brings me to one final point, James: And that is the attached evil, wretched, threatening letter [p. 135] that I received about a week ago from "one of Bill Clinton's closest childhood friends," Mark Mason in re my recent visit to Little Rock and the horrible fate that awaits me if I ever go back there—especially on election night, 41 days from now, which I definitely plan to do.

I'd hate to think that this ugly four-page threat actually speaks for the Clinton campaign, James. I don't want to go anywhere near that prison called Tucker Farm. And let me remind you that there are laws against kidnapping and brutalizing famous journalists—even if you are the next president. You could do that, but it would be wrong. Remember what happened to Tex Colson.... Indeed, putting me on a subhuman Arkansas chain gang might send a demoralizing message to many decent Americans of all ages, James, and would almost certainly get a Clinton administration off on a wrong karmic foot.

And who is fucking "Mark Mason" anyway? Aren't there also laws against impersonating a friend of the president and abuse of executive power? A dope-addled brother is one thing—but I brought the governor a fine #5 Vandoren saxophone reed; which was rudely received, at best, but it's no reason to put me in jail because Bill thought I was the ghost of Tommy Stukka. That is unacceptable.

In closing, let me direct your attention to my oddly incomplete hotel reservations (at the Capital) for November 2 through November 5. You'll note that election night, November 3, is missing—which is awkward, unless you people are planning some kind of raucous all-night celebration on a nearby riverboat, with top-deck suites reserved for selected journalists....

Perhaps you could help me straighten this out, James. I could easily get in trouble and end up on Tucker Farm if I got evicted from my room just for Tuesday night. I might not want to sleep, but I always need a place to hide.

Mark Mason

September 2, 1992

Dr. Hunter S. Thompson

Hotel Carlyle

New York City

Dr. Thompson:

I hope this letter reaches you in time, since your well-being may depend on whether you heed my warning before your next meeting with soon-to-be President Bill Clinton. The fact that you survived the Rolling Stone interview in Little Rock is a testament to Bill's self-control and to your continuing string of lucky breaks.

I grew up with Bill Clinton and, until he left for college, was one of his closest friends. I hope that what I am about to reveal will be of benefit to the both of you.

It is hard for me to describe the feeling I got when I saw the report on MTV announcing the Rolling Stone interview in Little Rock. It never dawned on me that you would ever come face to face with Bill, and to tell you the truth, it was not until I saw you sitting within two feet of him that I realized the true significance of this meeting.

As I said, Bill and I grew up in Hope, Arkansas, and were probably what you would call best friends. Being so close to Bill, I was privy to some of his innermost thoughts; his hopes and dreams, loves and hates. This personal knowledge of Bill is what caused me such great concern when I saw you sitting there next to him at Doe's.

You see, Dr. Thompson, you bear an uncanny resemblance to Bill's childhood nemesis, Tommy Stukka. Bill hated him with every fiber of his body, and with good reason. I had hoped that Tommy's death would enable Bill to put this to rest and get on with his life, but your meeting with him in Little Rock confirmed my worst fears... he never forgot. How do I know? By the look in Bill's eyes when he met you. You described that look exactly as I remember it, and I am surprised that you left Arkansas unscathed, nuts intact.

The Stukkas were a white-trash family of 12 who lived about a half mile from the Clintons, right next to the Cotton Belt Railroad tracks. The whole family lived in what used to be the Hope feed depot; the whole family, that is, except for Tommy.

Tommy was so mean and dirty that his own family wouldn't let him in the house. He slept on the back of an old Borden's milk truck that sat up on blocks in the backyard. The only thing that Tommy could call his was an old broke-dick dog that followed him everywhere and even slept with him. Tommy had that dog for six years and never even named it.

I remember when Tommy turned that dog loose on one of the pet rabbits that Bill brought to school for show-and-tell. The dog not only killed it, he ate the whole thing, including the ears. From that day forward, Bill was never to be the same again. In fact, I look back on that incident as one of the reasons that Bill is governor and will probably be president. It caused him to develop an inner meanness and thirst for revenge that is a prerequisite for politics in Arkansas.

There were other things that Tommy did that made Bill's life a living hell. Like calling him "niggerhead" because of Bill's naturally wiry hair or "pussylips" because of the exaggerated pout that Bill affects when hurt.

These taunts must have really hurt Bill. I recall years later, during his first term as governor, how he reacted upon hearing of Tommy's death. I remember him saying without a hint of emotion, "That's what he gets for trying to break into the State Police barracks." What he "got" was 18 pellets of .00 buck in the back. True, his body was found at the barracks, but people are still trying to figure out what the hell he was doing there.

What made all this so bad was the fact that Bill would not have turned out this way had it not been for the cruel treatment he suffered at the hands of this guy who, as genetics would have it, looked remarkably like you . . . even as a teenager.

I remember Bill as a genuinely sensitive young man who often spoke of marrying a nice girl, raising a family, and helping his fellow man. The day Bill met Hillary he called me and said that he had "just met the prettiest little thing" he had even seen. Although he didn't intimate it to me, it was apparent that he had come to know her carnally.

This was a significant event in Bill's life. Up until this point, as far as I know, his knowledge of sex had been limited to what he could coax out of the family's cheese goat, Sue-Sue. That, and his participation in what was almost a rite of manhood back then: "stumpin' Hitch."

Beginning in the spring of each year, a group of four of us would go over to Mr. Billups's farm and chase his mule "Hitch" around the pasture until he was too tired to run anymore. We would then lead him over to an old pine stump, where Bill would take over. Bill was big; even at thirteen he was the size of a full-grown man. I can still see Bill on that stump, ol' Hitch's tail between his teeth, just a tuggin' at that old blue gum mule's withers. Once he got him backed up just right, he would... maybe I shouldn't go into detail, since you are the only one to know about this besides us boys, and we damn sure ain't tellin'.

Anyway, back to this "look" I was talking about. The look on your face on page 55 of the September issue of Rolling Stone is revealing. It is the look of a man who is gripped by fear but unsure why. I don't know if it is your response to something Bill said or your reaction to that "look" that you described so well and that I have seen too many times. Whatever the cause, your reaction tells me this: Among the things you may have lost over the years, your instinct is not one of them. You knew, but did not know why.

Among other things you may or may not have known is just how close you came. Had you focused on Bill's hair a second too long or made a comment, even in passing, about the labial quality of his lips, you would most surely have sealed your fate.

What fate is that, you ask? There exists in Arkansas a prison known as Tucker Farm, where men toil in the mosquito-infested cotton fields by day and fashion anal bungs out of apple cores by night. I have a friend who spent time there a few years ago on a trumped-up drug charge.... To this day he has to wear one of those adult diapers to keep his small intestines from sliding down his pants leg when he laughs, which is not often.

Lest you doubt what I say, remember that this is the same man who had his own brother arrested and sent to prison in response to the public outcry that he was "soft" on drug users. Be warned that even aspirin require a prescription in Arkansas.

He only has power in one state now, and you can choose to stay away from there if you want. However, should he be elected president, I don't have to tell you that there will be no place for you to hide. Your options would number but two: plastic surgery or expatriotism; and even then you would not be assured safety.

I'm sure the question has crossed your mind: "Why didn't he just have me seized at Doe's?" This goes back to what I said about Bill's control; he realizes that the possibility of negative publicity generated by such a scene was too risky at this stage of the game. Besides, he doesn't think you suspect anything, and there is plenty of time to deal with you and the others after the election. Indeed, I myself run a great risk in writing this letter.

Bill holds a grudge, and while I'm sure he knows you are not really Tommy Stukka, you look enough like him to stir up old memories. Play it safe, Doc; stay away from that brute until I can talk to him and clear this up.

Cautiously yours,
Mark Mason

Fri 25 Sep 92 Magic Johnson quits AIDS Commission, saying Bush ignored commissions' recommendations

Fri 25 Sep 92 Reagan aide links Bush to Iran-contra—the former aide claimed that Bush knew about the arms-for-hostages arrangement in 1986, contradicting earlier Bush statement

Sat 26 Sep 92 CNN poll—Issues

Clinton and draft

He is lying	40%
He is not lying	7%
Not sure	23%

Bush and Iran-contra

He is lying	63%
He is not lying	22%
Not sure	15%

Want Perot back in Race?

Yes	**24%**
No	**66%**

09/25/1992 14:11 CNN ADMINISTRATION 404 523 8517 P.01

CNN

TURNER BROADCASTING SYSTEM, INC.
ONE CNN CENTER, Box 105366, Atlanta, GA 30348-5366

ED TURNER
Executive Vice President

SEPT 25

DEAR DOC:

BECAUSE THIS VERY DATE IS MY BIRTHDAY (RENTED, I COME FROM A POOR FAMILY), I AM GOING TO EXERCISE MY CONSIDERABLE INFLUENCE WITH THOSE REPRESENTING TRUTH, JUSTICE AND THE WALL STREET WAY (THE WHITE HOUSE) TO TRY AND KEEP THEM FROM DEPORTING YOU. NOW, WE MAY LOSE YOUR ANCILLARY RIGHTS SUCH AS VOTING, FREEDOM OF SPEECH, RIGHT TO OWN A FAX MACHINE AND CERTAINLY WHINING AND SNIVLING ATTRIBUTES FOUND ONLY IN LIBERALS LIVING AT HIGH ALTITUDES BUT TRY I SHALL. THERE IS A LEG OFF OUR FAX TO JAMES BAKER THE III 'S OFFICE AND HE IS DIFFICULT TO CALM DOWN AFTER YOUR MISSIVES; I MANAGED TO CONVINCE HIM NOT TO CALL AN AIR STRIKE ON OWL FARM, WHATEVER THAT IS (A COLLECTIVE FOR FEATHERY HOBOS FROM THE OREGON JUNGLE, ONE SUPPOSES) AND CONVERT YOUR WATER SUPPLY INTO A RUN-OFF FROM A NY DIOXIN PLANT. YOU ARE BEING SHIPPED A FEW THOUSAND KURDS WHO WERE SECRETLY LIVING IN THE DC SUBWAY SYSTEM BUT THERE IS NOTHING I CAN DO ABOUT THAT. TRY TO FEED THEM WEEKLY AND DROP A FEW MORTAR ROUNDS INTO THEIR CAMPSITES SO THEY WILL NOT GET HOMESICK. THE BEST LINE OF THE WEEK, SPOTTED BY ME DURING A RUSH THROUGH SAN ANTONIO, "[illegible] PEROT IS THE YELLOW ROSS OF TEXAS." IF GOVERNOR CLINTON SHOULD WIN--AND IT CERTAINLY LOOKS LIKE IT FROM HERE--YOU GET TO WRITE HIS SPEECHES. SEIZE THE MOMENT,ET

TOTAL P.01

TNT

Thanx

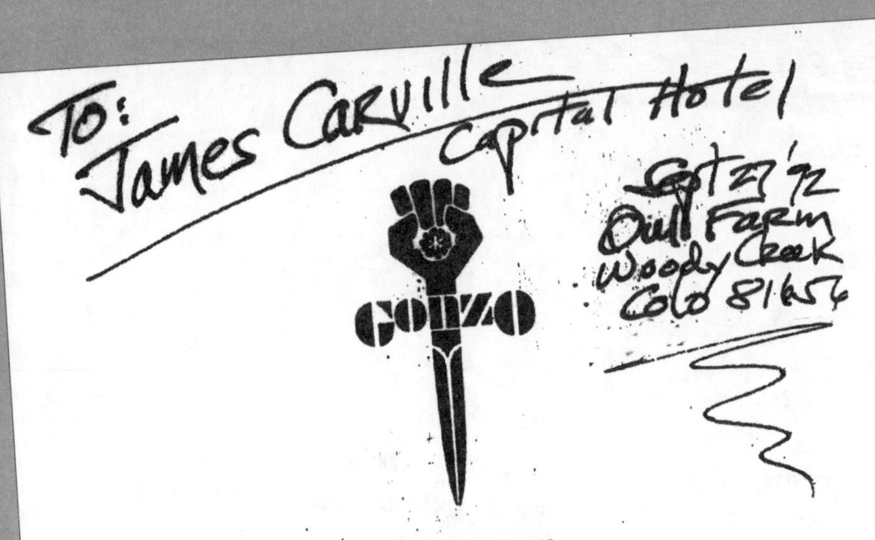

TO: James Carville
Capital Hotel
Sept 27 '92
Owl Farm
Woody Creek
Colo 81654
GONZO

AMENDMENT IV
to the U.S. Constitution

The right of the people to be secure in their persons, houses, papers, and effects, against unreasonable searches and seizures, shall not be violated, and no warrants shall issue, but upon probable cause, supported by oath or affirmation, and particularly describing the place to be searched, and the persons or things to be seized.

Dear James

Enc/below/pg ②
is a vital business
communication between
me + Ms. Clinton, re:
serious Literary action,
which I trust you will
hand to her ASAP. Thanx.

Please do it, James.
We will all be richer
+ happier for it.
Even you. Okay.

HST

Urgent Business Rush

ROLLING STONE

Dr. Hunter S. Thompson: National Correspondent

Sept 27 '92

Ms. Hillary Clinton

Clinton for President Hq. -- Little Rock, Ark

c/o James Carville, Capital Hotel

PERSONAL & CONFIDENTIAL

Dear Ms. Clinton:

Sorry I missed you on my recent trip to Little Rock, but we were forced to flee town because of rudeness.

We did okay -- in Retrospect but there was one conspicous failure, & it has haunted me ever since and now we must deal with it.

Before leaving for Little Rock, I promised my good friend & long-time Literary Agent, Lynn Nesbit, that I would swoop you up & bring you back to Manhattan on our huge golden jet and give you to her as a birthday present.

Please help me, Hillary. Lynn is vicious & beautiful & powerful -- but she scorns me now, because I failed.

Which is wrong, as we know, & I don't need it.... And neither do you, Hillary, so do us both a huge favor & turn all yr. literary affairs over to Lynn as soon as possible. Thanx.

-- 000 --

In closing, I remain yr. wise & faithful servant.

HST

Dr. Hunter S. Thompson

cc: Lynn Nesbit

Sept 28 '92

Owl Farm

To: Random House

I will fight for your right to be weird—just as I know you will fight for mine.

We may be weird, Bubba, but we are not as weird as George Bush. He is like a dying yellow dog with broken teeth and slits for eyes and nothing else to say. The evil brute is finished. He will flap around on the hook for a while—just another leader of the free world turned into a mass of foul jelly—but the minute he sinks below 30 percent in the polls (or when Clinton goes over 50 percent), he will start acting dangerously crazy and attack in every direction like a savage gut-shot hyena with only minutes to live. He is already trading strip-mining rights in 24 national forests for electoral votes in the Rust Belt, and he long ago peddled the remains of his wretched ass to a band of God-spewing religious Nazis and stupid hate-mongers. . . .

But all that is nothing compared to the horrible damage he'll do when he knows that his deal has finally gone down. It will be like George Wallace on his deathbed being told that his final appeal to go to heaven has been denied and that hell is run by a gang of mean niggers.

George Bush is doomed, along with all the rest of his rotten, degraded family. Shit. Even Nixon is stabbing him in the nuts. We are coming into the time of Mr. Bill, and many things will change very quickly without warning.

So be prepared; the last train from Little Rock has already left the station and the terrible night of the whore-hopper will come on November 3. Take my word for it. I understand these things and you don't.

And I will be there—to experience the final throes of this tragically sexualized presidential campaign that will mean the end for George Bush, Marilyn Quayle and many others. Beware. The time has come, Bubba. The hog is out of the tunnel and he can't be stopped.

Tue 29 Sep 92 Bush proposes debate dates during World Series

OCTOBER 1992

Thu 01 Oct 92	Citing pleas of volunteers, Perot reactivates campaign; names Admiral James B. Stockdale as his running mate
Thu 01 Oct 92	CNN tracking poll begins: Bush 35%, Clinton 52%, Perot 7%
Fri 02 Oct 92	U.S. missiles accidentally hit Turkish ship during training exercises

Oct 2, 92
Owl Farm

FORGET THE SHRIMP HONEY
I'M COMING HOME WITH THE CRABS

James Carville

Was George Bush a member of the horrible TAIL-HOOK Association? I heard he was, James — until last year, when the orgies finally got out of hand.

"Let's make the bastard deny it."
— LBJ, 1946

You're welcome, HST

VULTURES ATTACK FUNERAL—AND EAT THE CORPSE!

October 6, 1992

To: Johnny Cusak

You need a political movie? How about the story of an ex-president eaten by giant snails on the night of Xmas Eve, only 55 days after losing the election?

He was drunk with James Baker in the Lincoln Room—building a fire and finishing off his enemies list—when a huge pod of giant snails (hung in the chimney by Baker, for political reasons) suddenly burst open from the fire-heat, and thousands of hungry, gigantic, burning (or fire-molten), pansexual, constantly multiplying, meat-eating, savage, brainless, disease-bloated fiery monster snails erupted out of the Lincoln fireplace and swarmed over them before they could stagger to the door, which was locked anyway, from the outside, by somebody who was also gummed-up and eaten while screaming for help (in German) as flames engulfed the East Wing....

Whacko!!! How's that for a snail story, Bubba?

Remember The Blob when that horrible scum burst into the bowling alley?

Wonderful. But it was nothing compared to fiery snails coming down a chimney in the White House!

Huge box office, baffled critics, rave reviews in the highbrow press—"...the political movie of the decade."

It had to happen: "The Strange and Terrible End of the 'Reagan Revolution.'" Clinton laughs, Bush sues, Cusak arrested....

It will be the secret story of what really happened to the president and his trusted Judas goat in their desperate final hours—treachery, drunkenness, war against Turkey, nationwide police riot, palace revolt, botched military takeover, collapse of the dollar, wild whores in the streets....

Whoops! We don't want to tell the whole story, do we? You already have enough to get me $200K immediately, for fleshing out the narrative, as it were.

Okay. Let me know soonest—lest the story get stale in my brain. You can stay here if you bring enough money.

Thanx,

Doc

Wed 07 Oct 92 Bush charges Clinton with leading anti-American demonstrations in Moscow during sixties

10/7/92

To: George Stephanopoulos

Goddamnit, George:

How long do you giddy bastards think you can hang on to your "lead" by having Mr. Bill act more and more like George Bush?

Why the fuck are you on the defensive again? Bush should be attacked about these Sunday-night debates that he is jabbering about. Shit. That is a home-run ball; Bill should have bashed it straight out of the park by laughing at the brain-dead, out-of-touch, senile, dumb-rich, flat-out arrogance of any thin-blooded dingbat who wants to get me and my people into a string of cheap vaudeville-style political arguments when we're happily watching God-given sporting events.

What about those 100 million folks who might want to watch the World Series on Sunday night??? And the 55 million others who love Sunday Night Football??? Does he think they won't vote?

No! He doesn't give a damn about those people. He's been in hiding in the White House for so many years that he's even lost touch with football. He doesn't even watch the World Series!

What does he want to do: force 155 million sports fans who might also be good decent Americans—who might also plan to vote on November 3—to watch a goddamn silly, stage-managed political squabble every Sunday night from now until after Halloween? Why?

Instead of the World Series??? Instead of Dallas at Philadelphia??? Sheeeeit, is he nuts? Ho, ho.

Does he want to make all those folks choose, every Sunday night, between watching him doing his low-rent chicken-man dance once again—and then again and again and again—commanding a de facto blackout of all sports on Sunday night TV????

Is that it? Is he so dumb and so desperate and so doomed that he can't understand or maybe not even believe that democracy and the right to vote and the American dream can exist side by side with other basic rights like watching Sunday Night Football and the World Series on TV???

Life is grim enough in this country today—and George Bush takes credit for making it that way—without asking 110 million registered voters and sports fans to give up one of the few chances they have in these sleazy, humorless times to just lay back and enjoy something, to relax for a few hours without having to struggle with the tax man or the bill collector or a family crisis brought on by sudden money problems.

Is George Bush nuts! Does he think I don't watch the World Series? Or Sunday Night Football?

What does he watch on Sunday night? Jimmy Swaggart? Night Bankruptcy Court? Maybe he likes the Animal Kingdom reruns, or The Charles Manson Story...? It will not be 60 Minutes, for sure. George no longer watches the news, either.

Thu 08 Oct 92	**CNN tracking poll**	
	Bush	**34%**
	Clinton	**50%**
	Perot	**9%**

Oct 8, 1992

To: James Carville

Urgent

James:

Bush looked good on TV last night (Larry King from San Antonio), and Mr. Bill (in earlier news clips) looked like he might be a smart hillbilly with a bad temper.... Sort of like Uncle George appearing with his rebellious, favorite, half-smart nephew with more pimples than brains....

Here's Bush: "We all loved James Dean, folks—but we didn't elect him president, did we?" [Laughs condescendingly at Clinton, then turns his back on Bill and shakes his head sadly as he looks compassionately straight into the TV camera and crosses his eyes while making the sign of the fruit loop, moronically attempting to screw his left index finger into his brain and then winking brazenly into the eyes of 100 million suddenly interested voters who find themselves laughing out loud or at least giggling as they make the fruit loop at each other.]

Take my word for it, James: If Bush mentions James Dean, you're finished...unless, of course, Mr. Bill has enough sense of fun to grin at him and drop quickly into a sort of linebacker's crouch and make the sign of the stretched-wide mouth at Bush, which will almost certainly demoralize him, causing a loss of focus....

That's right, James: I have it all figured out—and if I had any

Owl Farm, Woody Creek, Colorado 81656

say in this thing I would make Bill practice both the sign of the fruit loop and the sign of the stretched-wide mouth, just in case Bush tries to get as cute and friendly and funny as he was on Larry King.... Don't let the laugh meter beat you on Sunday. Shit, all he needs is one. And then Bush will keep it coming! "James Dean wouldn't have qualified to fly a bomber in wartime—he couldn't even drive a car on a public highway at night without crashing into something and killing himself."

"It was horrible, folks. We all weep, even now, for the tragic death of James Dean.... I went into seclusion, as I recall—but not for long, because I was serving my country in Hong Kong; or was it Moscow? And where was Clinton?

"Who knows, folks? There was a war on—like we used to say in those dark, dangerous years before we finally won it! The Cold War. ¡No mas!

"That was last year, folks, only months ago, when I personally engineered and orchestrated our final, total victory over the once-invincible Russian bear and the cancer of Soviet communism.

"Not to mention our final solution to the global lifelong fear of sudden nuclear death at any moment, on any street corner, from a death-rain of huge bombs and nuclear missiles [pause, smiles] that no longer threaten us today—and which are being disarmed even now, as we speak with each other today [pause, smiles].

"And by the way, Bubba—where was Bill Clinton on the night James Dean died? Drunk and naked on some teenage golf course in Arkansas???

"Ripping lust-maddened tire tracks across the 18th green? Chasing a naked young girl into the woods?"

Think about it, James. You're lucky you ain't running against me. I would have that degenerate bastard locked up for his own good....

HST

FOURTH AMENDMENT FOUNDATION
405 South Presa Street
San Antonio, Texas 78205-3495
(512) 227-5311 FAX 227-6302

Owl Farm

To: Eli Segal

Clinton Headquarters

Dear Eli:

Mr. Bill needs a taste of the real thing. Prepare him for the worst—a snickering, condescending, long-suffering wise and war-weary commander in chief brought momentarily low by foreign bankers and somehow reduced to squabbling in public with some half-bright whacko kid from the Ozarks who didn't have the sense not to be photographed sharing a greasy, hand-rolled "American loco" cigarette with a scantily clad female KGB agent while necking openly in the shadow of Lenin's tomb.

Bush [sudden leering chuckle]: "... And let me tell you something, folks: The traditional communist ritual of kissing the bust of Lenin took on a whole new meaning that day! Wow! Talk about steamy photographs! You should have a look at these! [Suddenly whips a batch of grainy wax-paper fax photocopies out of his pocket and waves them in front of the camera, laughing harshly.]

"You know what I think of pornography, folks? How I've always handled obscenity? Just watch! [He flips open his silver White House Zippo and sets the filth on fire, then laughs and makes as if to toss the blazing heap into Clinton's lap, causing the Governor to recoil and squawk with fear....]

"Ho, ho. Don't be afraid, Billy. It's only fire [then holds it up like a magician and blows out the flames with one quick and powerful breath]—Wooof! Zoom! Gone. No more fire.

"How's that, Billy? Can you do that?" [Then throws back his head and flings out his arms and utters a wild wolflike scream of triumph and magic dominance that scares the shit out of 100 million people who will never forget the terrible sound and sight of it....]

Let's face it, Eli—the Governor would not be entirely at ease if a thing like that happened to him on national worldwide TV. He would probably go wild and smack Uncle George upside the head, then have to be restrained by Secret Service agents from stomping on him....

So I guess you see why I'm nervous about Sunday—especially when I see Bush regaining his sense of humor and Clinton getting edgy and smiling like a pit bull from time to time....

Remember this, Eli—Clinton is on his own turf this time. And Bush is so desperate that he'll even slink into Mr. Bill's Neighborhood and try to pick a fight.

Let's face it, Bubba: George Bush is a very successful man with many powerful friends in the business community—and on some days he can even be amusing—but he has been a genuinely rotten president of the United States and history will not be kind to him—or to us, either, if we shame ourselves by returning the new-rich inbred scum to another four years of plundering the national treasury and gutting the American Dream.... If they win, we lose. And the operative word here is we. Maybe Bill should use it more often. We is a very big word....

—HST

10 Oct. 1992

Hunter Threatens Move To Paraguay

LOUISVILLE, Ky. (AP) — Hunter S. Thompson says he expects Democrat Bill Clinton to win the White House this year. But if President Bush is re-elected, the gonzo journalist is moving to Paraguay.

Thompson, best known for his dispatches from the 1972 presidential campaign for Rolling Stone magazine, collected in the book "Fear and Loathing on the Campaign Trail," addressed a literacy group's fund-raiser Wednesday night.

He met recently with Clinton.

"I expect to win this time," said Thompson, a bottle of scotch and a garbage can filled with ice at his side.

"If we don't win, we're going to move Rolling Stone to Paraguay and have a colony down there," he said. "It's got the worst points of both (Brazil and Argentina) and none of the best. There's no place like it in the United States except maybe west Texas."

Thompson also suggested the nation's literacy rate has worsened during the Reagan-Bush years.

"It's been 12 years of the most oppressive, red neck, stupid ... greedhead politicians in this country," Thompson told about 1100 people at the fund-raiser in his hometown of Louisville for the Kentucky Foundation for Literacy.

Sun 11 Oct 92 **During the course of the debate, Bush comments that if reelected, Baker would handle domestic affairs. Clinton attacks Bush on his remarks about Clinton's patriotism, citing Bush's father as an example of acceptable behavior. Candidates exchange views on the economy.**

Tue 13 Oct 92 VP candidates—Dan Quayle, Al Gore and Admiral William Stockdale—debate in Atlanta

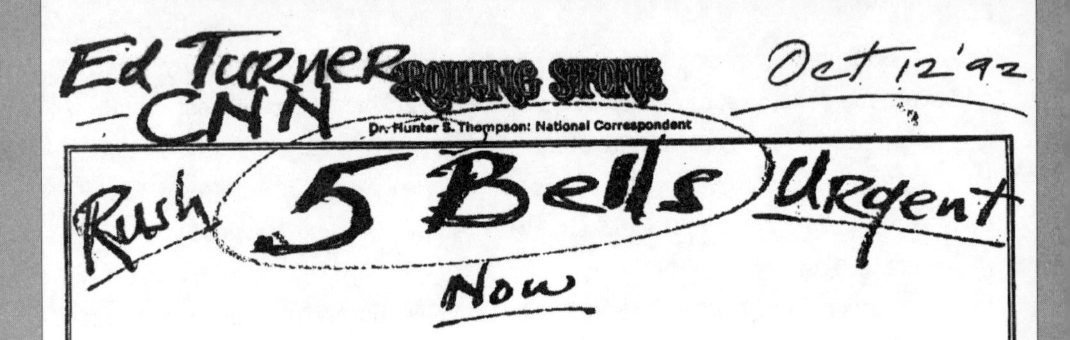

Ed Turner
— CNN
ROLLING STONE
Dr. Hunter S. Thompson: National Correspondent
Oct 12 '92
Rush
5 Bells
Urgent
Now

Dear Ed,

The word on the street is that the Bush/Baker/Perot axis has you in its grip, for some reason, and that they have a stranglehold on the jugular vein of CNN news focus.... It's horrible and wrong and I'm getting real tired of having to deny these stupid rumors about you.

And I have an idea, Ed—a way to crush all these sinister allegations with one elegant, super-patriotic stroke (that's super-patriotic stroke [sic]), to wit:

You should go on the air on Wednesday about 10:00 A.M. and call for Ross Perot to withdraw from the race at once (and quit the debate on Thursday night) if he really believes in the American political process, like he says he does—and if he hasn't been a hired creature of James Baker 3 all along, a tool of the age-old divide-and-conquer strategy that will reelect George Bush. Horrible, horrible—but it's true, and you are the dupe who turned the public tide in favor of the shadowy B/B/P axis and "went along with it"—for one reason or another (ho, ho)—and then resigned his news job (very graciously) when word got out that he was going to be the next ambassador to the Court of St. James.... It was a sure thing—

Until he was smeared, somehow (in a "drug scandal connection" with rock 'n' roll or sex freaks), and was cruelly passed

Owl Farm, Woody Creek, Colorado 81656

over for the St. James gig and eventually found employment with an obscure radio station in Oklahoma. . . .

No, Ed—don't let that happen to you again. If only because it will make it easier for me to get my hands on you, on my journey to my new home in Paraguay (where I have, in fact, already been offered a major position in our embassy in '93).

My only real fear is that they will renege on the offer and force me to stay in this country if you and your people get your way and get Bush reelected. . . .

And if that happens, Ed—I'll be coming to you, on some snow-blind midnight in Oklahoma, for refuge and gainful employment and protection from my enemies.

That is the nut of it, Ed. That is what will happen if you don't go on the air tomorrow and call for Perot to drop out of the race immediately—so the American people can really have their say, one on one, instead of being led astray by the hired-gun diversions of the Perot fraud.

He is not one of us, Ed. He is a giddy little state-socialist who became feverishly addicted to the sight of himself on TV—and who will reelect George Bush if he doesn't get out of the race tomorrow (for "high patriotic reasons," of course—near "preterhuman self-sacrifice") and let the people decide.

In the end, he will be seen as a hero. Hell, you can convince him of that, eh? Yeah. Sure you can. Do it for us, Ed. Do it for Jane and Ted, and do it because it's right.

Okay. Let me know if I can be of any assistance.

HST

** → MARY

*

see following page two (2) FAX to Ed Turner/CHX1

GONZO

Oct 12 '92
Owl Farm

JANN

The time has come for YOU to speak out (on the AIR — have a press conference at YR. Office) and Call for Perot to Withdraw from the Race (+ the Debates) at Once — because he will re-elect George Bush if he doesn't

(+1)

An Actual Transcript: A PHONE CONVERSATION

HST to JD office of George Stephanopoulos

HST Hi, Jackie. This is Hunter Thompson here.

JD Hi. How are you?

HST Well, I'm a little bit weird here. Because I've been involved in this strange negotiation with Ed Turner.

JD With Ted Turner?

HST This is ED Turner, who's the VP of all news at CNN. And Ted is the…we know Ted. Ed is the power behind the scenes. I know it sounds weird, but it's true. They're not related.

JD What can I do for you?

HST Well, I'm trying to get this thing through to George, because apparently Ed is going to go on the air today or tomorrow and call for the withdrawal of Perot.

JD Okay.

HST Yeah, I've been involved in this talk with him and—did you get that stuff I sent through to George earlier?

JD The fax? Yes, I did.

HST We should probably get it to him, because it involves what I'm sending you right now. This is a response from Ed Turner at CNN.

JD So, Ed Turner is going to go on the air and encourage Mr. Perot to drop out of the race?

HST Well, that's what I'm talking to him about, yeah. I'm not sure it's a—

JD —Now, you're encouraging this or he's offering this?

HST Well, the fax I'm going to send you indicates that he's thinking about doing it today or tomorrow.

JD I'm sorry. So, you're encouraging Ed Turner to go on the air and say this, or he's offering to go on the air and say this?

HST Well, the fax I sent to George there explains how this came about and also, Jann Wenner of Rolling Stone is doing the same thing. But I'm going to send you the response from Ed Turner to me, right now on the fax. If you give it to George, I think he'd really, I don't know, if nothing else, appreciate it.

JD Okay, great. I'll get it to him right away.

10/12/92

George:

I have had a wonderful response from Ed Turner/CNN, in re Perot quitting the race tomorrow.

He appears to be ready to act, George—and I'm still trying to bring you into the loop.

Why are your people so disorganized?

R.S.V.P.

Doc/Hunter

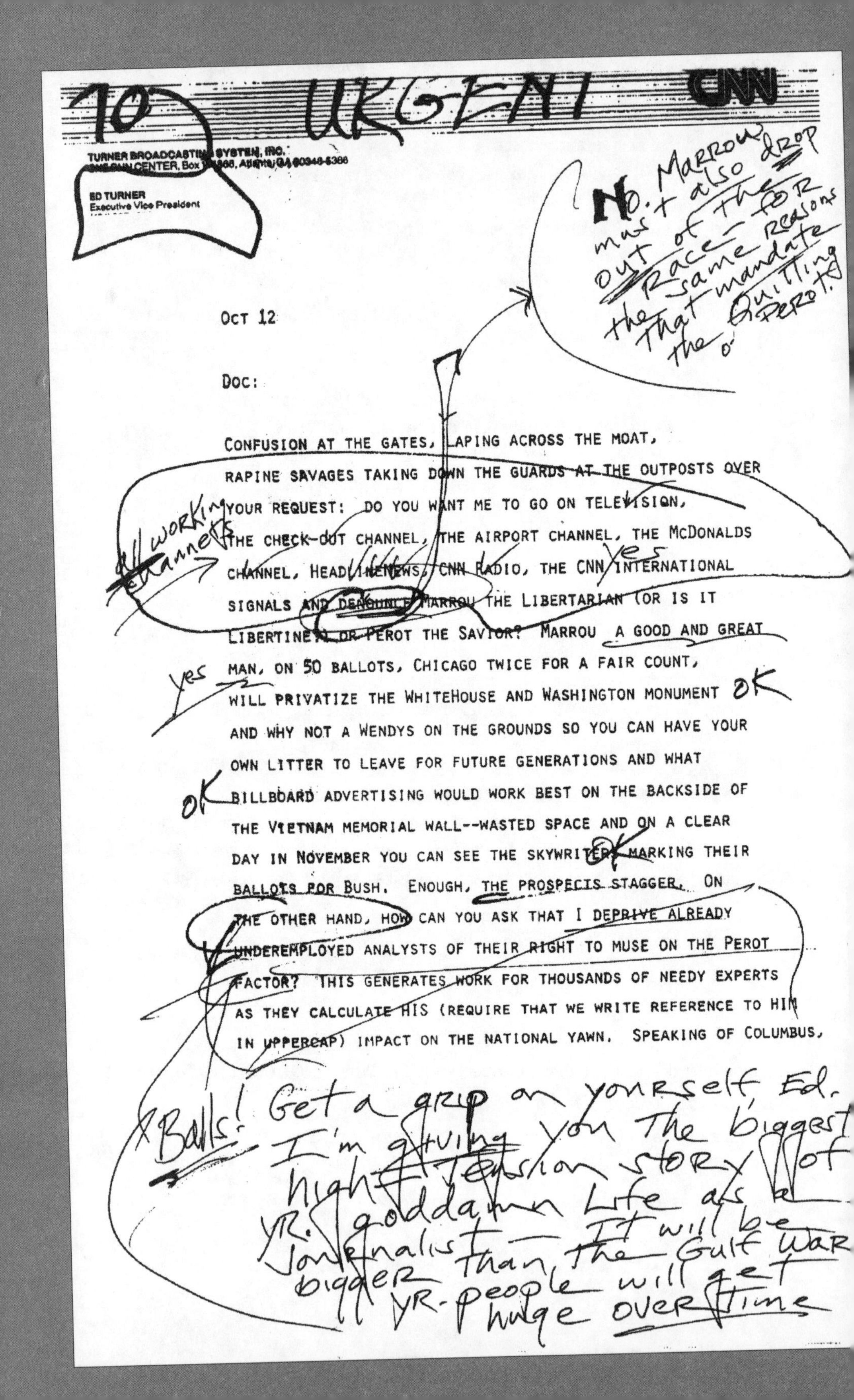

10 URGENT CNN

TURNER BROADCASTING SYSTEM, INC.
ONE CNN CENTER, Box 105366, Atlanta, GA 30348-5366

ED TURNER
Executive Vice President

OCT 12

DOC:

CONFUSION AT THE GATES, LAPING ACROSS THE MOAT, RAPINE SAVAGES TAKING DOWN THE GUARDS AT THE OUTPOSTS OVER YOUR REQUEST: DO YOU WANT ME TO GO ON TELEVISION, THE CHECK-OUT CHANNEL, THE AIRPORT CHANNEL, THE MCDONALDS CHANNEL, HEADLINENEWS, CNN RADIO, THE CNN INTERNATIONAL SIGNALS AND DENOUNCE MARROU THE LIBERTARIAN (OR IS IT LIBERTINE?) OR PEROT THE SAVIOR? MARROU A GOOD AND GREAT MAN, ON 50 BALLOTS, CHICAGO TWICE FOR A FAIR COUNT, WILL PRIVATIZE THE WHITEHOUSE AND WASHINGTON MONUMENT AND WHY NOT A WENDYS ON THE GROUNDS SO YOU CAN HAVE YOUR OWN LITTER TO LEAVE FOR FUTURE GENERATIONS AND WHAT BILLBOARD ADVERTISING WOULD WORK BEST ON THE BACKSIDE OF THE VIETNAM MEMORIAL WALL--WASTED SPACE AND ON A CLEAR DAY IN NOVEMBER YOU CAN SEE THE SKYWRITERS MARKING THEIR BALLOTS FOR BUSH. ENOUGH, THE PROSPECTS STAGGER. ON THE OTHER HAND, HOW CAN YOU ASK THAT I DEPRIVE ALREADY UNDEREMPLOYED ANALYSTS OF THEIR RIGHT TO MUSE ON THE PEROT FACTOR? THIS GENERATES WORK FOR THOUSANDS OF NEEDY EXPERTS AS THEY CALCULATE HIS (REQUIRE THAT WE WRITE REFERENCE TO HIM IN UPPERCAP) IMPACT ON THE NATIONAL YAWN. SPEAKING OF COLUMBUS,

No. Marrow must also drop out of the race—for the same reasons that mandate the quitting of Perot.
all working channels
yes
yes
OK
OK
OK
Balls! Get a grip on yourself, Ed. I'm giving you the biggest television story of yr. goddamn life as a journalist — It will be bigger than the Gulf War. Yr. people will get huge overtime

my grandfather was Korean, Ed

~~BEST NEW ACRONYM TO SURFACE AS YOUR CROWD EFFORTS HISTORY~~ 128 I
RE-WRITE IS DWEM--DEAD WHITE EUROPEAN MALE--AND DON'T THINK
WE WILL STAND DOWN FOR THIS. A LITTLE SLAVERY AND IMPORTED
HERPES IS ~~SMALL ENOUGH TO PAY FOR CIVILIZATION~~. ADVISE SOONEST
ON MARROU OR PEROT BUT BE PREPARED FOR EARTH PLATES TO MOVE.
SEIZE THE MOMENT,
ET

11 ST

Oct 12 '92

HUNTER

Squash them both — but
guarantee them Good
Jobs in Govt. in '93
give Marrou Total
Diplomatic Immunity &
make Perot Secretary
of HEW, Commerce,
State & Drug Czar
all at once... He
will Rise to The Challenge
& get out of our
goddamn way.

You can Do it Ed. And
you will be honored in
History as a Super-patriot

TOTAL P.02

Trust me! Ed.
Perot is a Mole for Bush
& Marrou is probably a
champion of fun & a
fine drinking companion
— But so what.
They must Go.
NOW! Yes
Do it! Ed

HST

URGENT Bulletin

ROLLING STONE

Oct 12 '92

Dr. Hunter S. Thompson: National Correspondent

To: James Carville (RUSH)

why did you let that goddamn little weasel into The "Debates" in the first place?

Fuck Ross Perot. He is an evil, dangerous TAR-Baby + The Willing Creature of James Baker 3, who wants to BURY us All. Especially you + Me. James. Trust me: I understand these things.

you're welcome,

HST

3

Owl Farm, Woody Creek, Colorado 81656

ROLLING STONE

Dr. Hunter S. Thompson: National Correspondent

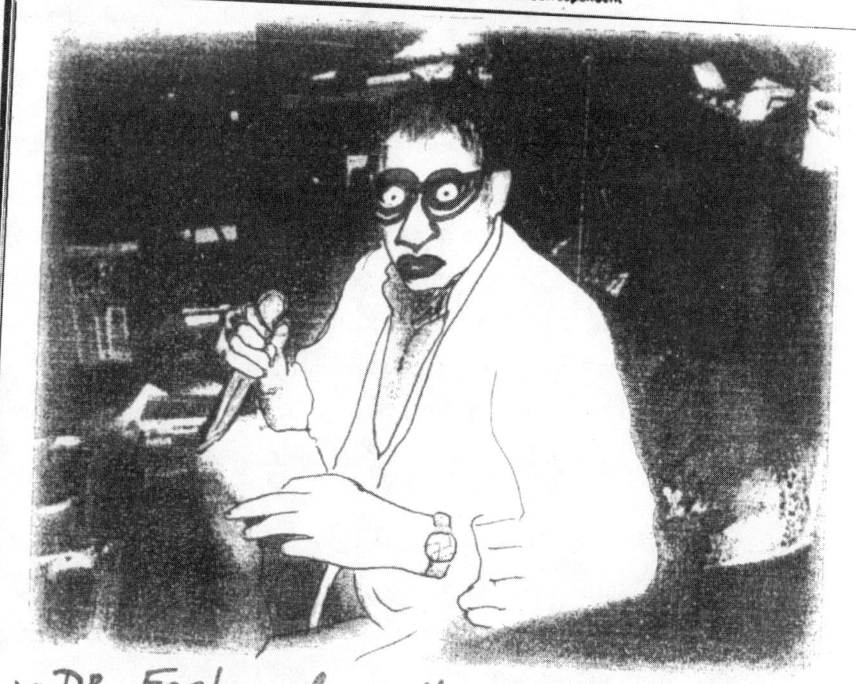

~DR. Feelgood will see you now~

To: James Carville/Capital Hotel/ Little Rock/10-14-92

From: HST/Woody Creek, Colorado

Subject: Crisis politics and the wisdom of LBJ

Comments: See below

Cheer up, James. This is the passing lane, and on some days it gets real narrow.... Hell, the scum always rises when the water gets hot. They are mean and rich and greedy and bloated with hate and fear after 12 years of power and excess profits. And they will rage against the dying of the light.. This is a

Owl Farm, Woody Creek, Colorado 81656

bad crowd, James, and too many of them would kill to be winners.... We are coming down to some very fast days, no matter what happens.... They are liars and thieves and forgers and fixers and pimps and slick-living power-junkies who are suddenly confronted with the end of the world as they know it.

So be careful who you drink with for the next few days. They might hire some treacherous freak to flatter you at the hotel bar and then stab you full of enough sedatives so they can drag you to some born-again tattoo parlor in an airstream on the outskirts of town and carve the sign of the Manson family on your forehead and weird Jap swastikas all over your back and then put you on a (private) plane to Dallas, stark naked and utterly crazy on truth serum for a god-awful photo-op and rabid confession in the blazing sun on the tarmac, just in time for the evening news and tomorrow's papers....

Hideous, eh? But it won't happen that way, James. It will probably be worse. They might hire Bill's daughter to say he abused her. Like Woody Allen...Or they might offer you $11 million in a brown bag and a diplomatic post in the Congolese Republic.

Ah, but I digress, James—and I figure you know all these things, anyway.... All I really wanted to tell you was this ancient and honorable story about how Lyndon Johnson first got elected to Congress, when his (heavily favored) opponent was a wealthy local pig farmer....

Remember that one, James? Sure you do. It's a wonderful story, and I suspect it will cheer you up.

It goes this way: The year was 1948, as I recall, and Lyndon was running about 10 points behind, with only nine days to go.... He was sunk in despair. He was desperate. And it was just before noon on a Monday, they say, when he called his equally depressed campaign manager and instructed him to call a press conference at two or two-thirty (just after lunch on a slow news day) and accuse his high-riding opponent (the pig farmer) of having routine carnal knowledge of his barnyard sows, despite the pleas of his wife and children....

His campaign manager was shocked. "We can't say that, Lyndon," he said. "It's not true."

"Of course it's not," Johnson barked at him, "but let's make the bastard deny it."

It works every time, James—even on smart people. And remember: You are running against (at least) two king-hell Texas politicians who don't mind saying that they didn't get where they are by telling the truth or being nice to people. They have controlled the most powerful office in the history of the world (sic) for 12 years, and they don't want to give it up.... Shit, why should they? Baker and Bush, between them, have washed enough human blood off their hands to stock the plasma banks of most small-town hospitals, and they are no longer spooked at the smell of it.

They would torture the queen of England for three days and nights to make her say that Bill Clinton raped her repeatedly while he was a student at Oxford and she has many crazed love letters to prove it. They are scum.

By the way, James—Lyndon won that election by something like 44 votes.

So don't let it happen to you. Don't deny anything—especially if they accuse you of fucking pigs.

Just stand up in front of the mike and smile like a champion and tell this good old classic LBJ story.... It's pure. There's no way to respond to it. Right: "What is this, Mr. Bush? More of your sleazy hired gossip? Good God, George! How low will you <u>crawl</u>?" Ho, ho.

Wed 14 Oct 92	U.S. embassies in Oslo and London were reportedly ordered to search their records for any information about Bill Clinton while he was a student in England. The Clinton campaign is reportedly outraged at the searches, calling them "part of a McCarthyite smear effort."
Thu 15 Oct 92	CNN tracking poll: Bush 32% Clinton 47% Perot 15%
Thu 15 Oct 92	Second presidential debate held in Richmond, Virginia
Mon 19 Oct 92	Third presidential debate held in East Lansing, Michigan

Thu 22 Oct 92	**CNN tracking poll:** **Bush 32%** **Clinton 44%** **Perot 17%**

ROLLING STONE

Dr. Hunter S. Thompson: National Correspondent

10-28-92
Owl Farm

To

Eli

Segal
— Little Rock
— in re: Clinton on Larry King — wed nite

tell the Gov. to Slow Down

OR

at least Breathe between para-grafs

He's right but he's making people nervous

Do it now!

OK,
Hunter

Owl Farm, Woody Creek, Colorado 81656

Jann,

I guess it won't surprise you to know that I've been for Perot all along—working for him, in fact—and everything I've done or said or tried in the past six months has been part of a master plan that I wanted to tell you about, but I couldn't... and I still can't. Not now...but soon. Maybe in the terrible chaos of Little Rock. Maybe in Washington. Who knows?

All I can tell you now, for sure, is that the master plan is so fine and smart and stunningly powerful that I know you will feel joy when it's finally made clear to you.... And don't worry about all this "Clinton" business; you meant well, and that will be remembered.

Right. And what else can I say, Bubba? Shit. I've been saying it all along. I've been trying to tell you, but you giggled and shrugged it off. I did everything possible (under the circumstances) to bring you into the loop—but you said it was all "irrelevant." Just a bunch of funny stories.

Right. Ho, ho.... Hang on to your sense of humor and drink a lot of whiskey.

Remember that I am your friend, Jann, and I have handled this thing pretty well....

Which is true. I have been wise and shrewd and suave—and, as a result, you were spared the fate of a doomed roach in the middle of a bowling alley at midnight. Or sheep in the savage harvest...

(Whoops! Nevermind sheep and roaches. We were talking about Bubba Ross and I guess I got sidetracked.... Fuck those people. And remember this: Baker 3 created Perot 2. They've been working together from the start... and now it's the whipsaw for Mr. Bill.)

Ye fucking gods! CNN says his lead is "down to single digits" (sic), eight points...he's lost 10 points in 10 days. And there's 10 more days to go. Think about it. The hog is out of the tunnel....

...O God, Jann! I can't go on.

And now Larry King is hosting Barbara Bush again.... (Larry is in on it, too—all along, from the start: He will be director of White House Communications before Groundhog Day. Take my word for it.)

And Baker 3 will be running the White House by July 4. That is the plan—which also involves massive fixing of the electoral college.

Thu 29 Oct 92	*New York Times* reports three polls:			
		Los Angeles Times	ABC News	NBC/*Wall Street Journal*
		Oct. 25–26	Oct. 26–27	Oct. 27
	Bush	34%	35%	36%
	Clinton	44%	42%	43%
	Perot	18%	20%	15%
Fri 30 Oct 92	New charges against Weinberger in Iran-contra, memo reveals Bush involvement			
Sat 31 Oct 92	**CNN tracking poll:**			
	Bush	**39%**		
	Clinton	**42%**		
	Perot	**14%**		

10/28/92

I'm leaving tonight (now/midnight) for Little Rock and expect to arrive Thursday night at the Capital Hotel, to do my work.

How about dinner?

If I drive like a bastard I can be there by 6:00 P.M. (Thursday night). I'll call you from the road—mainly I-40 through Amarillo.

I also have lawyers alerted in every town along the way—but don't worry: I am clean like the driven snow.

Which doesn't mean that some hophead freak of a cop in Fort Smith who loves Jesus and hates bald people might not try to fuck with me because of my religious beliefs....

I am driving a gold 1976 Fleetwood Eldorado Cadillac V-8 500 c.u. convertible with Colorado license plates—which I plan to auction off in Little Rock....

Try <u>that</u> for karma in the Ozarks.

So what? We are warriors—but unless CNN stops running these shit-eating yellow-press polls about a two-point spread, we may have a long night in Little Rock.

But what the hell? Two points is as good as 20 in this game, eh? Fuck Bush. He'll be lucky if the White House is all he loses next year.... If he wins he'll be impeached by the summer of '94 and Mr. Bill can run against Quayle next time.

Shit, James—you win either way.

Congratulations.

See you tomorrow.

Doc H

PART TWO

CHAPTER 8
HALLOWEEN IN LITTLE ROCK

Election night in the armpit of the Ozarks... Strange rumble with Carville, white slavery on the Gold Coast...Dead Cadillacs and dumb cocksuckers—it's all downhill from here...

> **In an age that is utterly corrupt, the best policy is to do as others do.**
>
> **— Marquis de Sade, 1788**

THE 1976 FLEETWOOD Eldorado Cadillac convertible is a monument to some of the ugliest moments in American history—the cruel and terrible journeys by mule trains and wagons and drag-sleds and wooden-wheeled "stage coaches" that hauled the great Westward Movement for 2,000 miles from the Mississippi River to the Rockies and on to California, where money grew on trees and the streets of San Francisco were paved with gold bricks.

Some people made it the easy way—taking six- or eight-month journeys on wooden steam-sailboats around the bottom of Argentina between icebergs and sea-monsters and shipwrecks in the frozen Strait of Magellan—where they had to stay well clear of any ice floe or island where they might be lured ashore by false land lights and then boarded at night by gangs of desperate, malaria-crazed survivors of some previous disaster who had been stranded there for nine months with no matches or water and only dead seal blubber to feed on while they waited with sharp sticks and bludgeons for the next ship to come through and maybe pick them up—and then up the other side, another 8,000 miles, past Chile and Lima and Mexico in a boat full of crazy people until they finally found the channel into San Francisco Bay and then swarmed frantically ashore, only to be set upon by cruel thugs and robbers who worked the waterfront in gangs that murdered the strong ones and sold the women and children into slavery on Chinese merchant junks, which carried them off another 6,000 miles to spend the rest of their lives in bamboo cages on the other side of the world.

The hard way to "go West" in America was to do it by land and creep across the continent at one or two miles a day and know that at any moment you might be scalped for no reason, or burned at the stake by Comanches, or maybe chopped up and eaten by your own traveling companions if you got trapped in the snow on a lonely pass above Reno, or forced to embrace cannibalism yourself.

THE 1976 CADILLAC is a monument to all these agonies, because it can take two people from St. Louis to San Francisco, in total climate-controlled comfort, in less than 48 hours with no problem worse than a few traffic tickets or getting raped in some motel parking lot. It is a land yacht, a luxury cabin on wheels, with a 500-cubic-inch V-8 engine and a vastly overrated "front-wheel drive." It weighs about three tons "fully loaded," and will take you anywhere you want to go in fine style at 100 miles an hour. The Fleetwood Eldorado is the final word in cruising.

That is why I decided to drive mine from Woody Creek, Colorado, to Little Rock, Arkansas, to be a part of Bill Clinton's victory celebration on the eve of the recent general election. What the hell? It was only about 1,200 miles—downhill, more or less—and the car was a subtle green-gold color that was not likely to attract much attention on the cop-infested highways of

Colorado, New Mexico, Texas, Oklahoma and Arkansas. We could make the journey in relative peace and comfort, without the ever-cheapening rigors of airbus and airport travel.

Nicole was not optimistic about loading up the Cadillac and driving 1,200 miles through hostile territory, just to get to Little Rock. "Why not just fly to Memphis and rent a car?" she said. "We could get there in four hours, instead of four days."

"Nonsense," I said. "It's an overnight trip. Once we get to Texas, it's a straight shot all the way to Little Rock. And remember, this is a very fast and extremely comfortable car."

"What if it breaks down?" she muttered. "Or you get us arrested in the middle of Oklahoma?"

"Don't worry," I said. "I have criminal defense lawyers alerted in every town between here and Little Rock. They are the best in the business."

"What?" she said. "You've hired *lawyers*?"

"Of course not," I said. "These people are my *friends*. They are the midnight warriors of the Fourth Amendment Foundation, and they are everywhere. We are guaranteed safe passage."

Nicole pleaded. "This car is cursed..."

"I know," I said. "But I swore I would drive it to Little Rock and give it to Clinton. It's a present to him from the Indian."

"Oh, no!" she said. "What Indians? Who owns the car?"

"Earl," I said. "But don't worry. It's in perfect shape."

"Are you crazy?" she said. "Earl is *wanted* in fourteen states!" She pointed at the Cadillac. "Look at the plates. We can't drive this car *anywhere*!"

The New Mexico license plate said DIE U PIG. It was one of those "personalized" things that cost a hundred dollars for seven digits, no questions asked. At least not at the courthouse.

But what happens when you run a red light in Amarillo and get pulled over by a Texas Ranger? Would he be offended by your DIE U PIG *plate? It was possible.*

But not if you handled it suavely: "Hi, officer. I see you're staring at my license plate, but it's not what you think. I'm a foreigner in my heart...born in Germany a long time ago....You bet, but I still remember the language, and I still respect it.You know what that license plate says in German? It says 'colorblind.' Yes, I'm colorblind. But only at night." Yeah. Ho, ho.

"Let's get those plates off the Chevy," I told Nicole. "It won't make any difference. Hell, they're both convertibles." Which was true, so we switched the plates and left for Little Rock at midnight on Monday.

Unfortunately, the huge Cadillac's brake cylinder blew out on the way to Denver, and our plans were changed dramatically. We abandoned the car on a side street and hailed a cab for the airport, where I chartered a Lear jet to Little Rock for five or six thousand dollars and charged it to my attorney, Michael Stepanian, who was in Bali at the time.

We touched down in Little Rock around 7:00 or 7:15, right on schedule, and went straight to the Capital Hotel. Our pilot had driven us into town in a borrowed van with a faulty tailgate that collapsed as he was unloading our mass of luggage and heavy equipment, hurling him headfirst down the street with an eerie scream that brought people running out of the lobby to help us—or maybe kill us. Who knows? I have never been at the Capital Hotel when it wasn't crawling with U.S. Secret Service agents. They have been there for most of the year: When it wasn't Bill Clinton or Hillary to protect, it was Big Al Gore, or Tipper, or Lynn Martin, or General Schwarzkopf for the sumo wrestling championship.

The Capital Lounge was crowded, but there was not enough tension, none of the cranked-up energy that you normally find in bars and elevators and hotel lobbies along the campaign trail.... It was hard to know that you were in the hot center of a winning presidential campaign—the hometown headquarters of a local boy who was about to become the next president of the United States.

That is big, Bubba—very big if you live in Washington—but it wasn't real big in Little Rock. It took me a few days to understand this: In Little Rock, the governor of Arkansas is bigger than the president of the United States. Washington is too far away to take seriously, but the governor's mansion is right across the goddamn street. It is where the boss lives—where the Clintons had lived for 10 years—and if the boss wanted to go off to Washington, the feeling in Little Rock was that he was probably taking a demotion.

The action picked up on the weekend, as busloads of gawkers and thrill-seekers began to drift in from Memphis and Hot Springs; occasionally there would be a crowd from St. Louis. There were also lawyers and lobbyists and a growing number of people who looked like they were from the Hamptons, or maybe

Georgetown. . . . They were fixers and Bubbas and job-seekers with slick-looking political wives who seemed vaguely amused at being crowded into the same rural cocktail lounge with half-naked Clinton staffers and Swedish journalists wearing I FUCKED GENNIFER FLOWERS T-shirts. It was an odd mix of people, but very calm and focused. There were no crazies—except maybe for me, and I wasn't having much fun. But I tried to make the best of it.

I am well known at the Capital Hotel and I have many friends on the staff. They were nervous at first, remembering the bad scene I made two months before in the lobby when they couldn't get a wheelchair and some morphine fast enough for my crippled friend Dollar Bill Greider, who was suffering visibly as we wheeled him into the lobby on a brass-railed baggage cart and blundered into a cordon of Secret Service bodyguards around Marilyn Quayle as she marched in her queenly fashion across the tiles of the hushed lobby on her way from the elevator to Ashley's black-tie restaurant, where she would dine alone, that night, far from the madding crowd of (Arkansas) GOP county chairmen (and chairwomen) who had gathered to pay homage.

Ah, but that was *last* time, when the Quayles still had some clout and some half-bright teenage dream of a political future. . . . Dan is, after all, the vice president of the United States, and his wife is a friend of Engelbert Humperdink's. That should count for something, these days—even in Little Rock.

But it doesn't. On any day in the week before Election Day, Marilyn Quayle could have floated stark naked on a pink inner-tube under both bridges in downtown Little Rock without attracting more attention than a pervert in the bushes near River-front Park.

THE LOBBY WAS FULL of pimps, journalists and Secret Service agents when we finally arrived. I paid Leon $200 in cash to haul our 900 pounds of loose-wrapped, high-tech luggage up to the room. He was a waterhead, so I sent him up the back way on a freight elevator and told Nicole to watch him carefully whenever he touched our bags.... "I think Leon is a cop," I told her. "He probably doesn't even work here, but we still have to humor him. That's why I gave him those hundred-dollar bills."

"You fool!" she said. "We're an hour late for dinner with Carville and you're already stupid drunk. I can't stand it. Get away from me. Go to the bar. Read a newspaper and don't talk to anybody. I'll get us checked in, then I'll—" She suddenly stiffened.

"Oh my God," she hissed. "There's James! Don't let him see you. Get out of sight, quick!"

I saw Carville hunched over a telephone at the front desk, laughing and muttering distractedly. "James!" I shouted. "What's happening?"

He grinned and waved me over. "Hot damn!" he said. "Crazy George just called the Larry King show and got straight through to Bush. He said he was Caspar Weinberger and threatened to commit suicide if Bush didn't stop lying."

"What?" I said. "Stephanopoulos did that? Tonight?"

He looked up from the phone and sneered at me. "No," he said. "He did it tomorrow." Then he laughed bitterly and waved me off.

"The Doc says you're crazy," he said into the telephone. "The Doc says you should be fired." He laughed and rolled his eyes at me, making a throat-slitting gesture. "You stupid little bastard!" he snarled at the phone. "You just blew the election!" He hung up and walked away. "I feel sick," he muttered. "I should have fed that Greek to the alligators a long time ago. I'm going up to my room. See you for dinner in a few minutes."

I shrugged and went into the bar. It was crowded, but I found a seat next to the huge marble centerpost, trying to stay out of sight.... Nicole had disappeared with the waterhead cop. The bitch has turned on me, I thought; I'm about to be busted and locked up.

Just then I noticed a slick-looking blond woman making a lewd signal at me from far across the bar. Then she smiled and blew me a kiss.

Ye gods, I thought. What now? She looked like Gennifer Flowers, and she was sitting next to a man who looked like a rich and mean drunk. I ignored her and tried to read the sports section, but I couldn't relate to it. There were too many politicians in the room.

The woman was smiling at me again, hoisting her snifter and fixing me with a stare that told me instantly that my life was about to turn weird. This one was clearly active.

I more or less instinctively returned her lewd salutation with a professional smile and a quick nod, then I turned to speak with the bartender.

"Welcome back, Dr. Thompson," he said. "Good to have you back with us." He slid a tall margarita across the bar and grinned at me. "It's amazing. Really amazing."

I became quickly alert, remembering the warning I'd received from Mark Mason. "Amazing?" I said. "Why? Did you think I was dead?"

"What?" he blurted. "Dead? Of course not, sir." He backed slightly away from me. "I just mean I never thought we'd see you back here in Little Rock again. Not after what happened last time."

His face remained solemn and respectful, but somebody to the left of me snickered, and I thought I heard laughter behind me. It was hard to tell. Then I heard a woman laughing, and I glanced down the bar to where the slick-looking blond woman was sitting—but she was gone.

I looked around me and everything seemed to be wrong—the laughter, the woman, the guilty-acting bartender and probably all the people behind me.

Suddenly, I felt a hand on my shoulder and then a person muscling their way into the cramped space between me and the marble pillar. . . .

It was a rude move in any bar; but it was also very suave and quick. "Hi," she said. "Do you mind if I shake your hand? You're my hero."

I knew who it was, and so did her mean, drunk, boyfriend,

who was watching us intently from his seat across the bar. . . . The bartender was bringing me another margarita as the woman was saying, "This is really incredible! I can't believe it's happening! I'm finally meeting my *hero*! I feel like swooning in your arms. . . ."

Whoops, I thought. Watch out! Something weird is happening here, and everybody's in on the joke except me.

"I'm Maureen," she whispered. "I adore you." She pulled me against her and buried her head on my chest. I rolled back against the bar, and people moved quickly aside to give us more room to nuzzle and coo and neck like the long-lost passion-crazed dream lovers that we seemed to be.

"You remind me of Emerson," she said. "I've always compared you to Emerson. . . ." She looked softly up into my eyes and suddenly I felt a hand sliding playfully across the front of my pants.

"I know why you're here," she said, "and I think you're going to need help. You can't do it alone in this town. It's too damn mean."

I nodded solemnly and called the bartender for another margarita. "One or two, Doc?" he asked, nodding at Maureen. "Three," I said. The place was filling up and getting very busy. The noise level was so high that I had to lean very close to her head to hear what she was saying. She put her arm around my waist and pulled me closer. I could feel the heat of her belly against mine, and she smiled as my arm brushed her nipples when I reached between us to get my Dunhills off the bar.

"I love crowds," she whispered. "I love to be crushed."

Ye gods, I thought. Nicole could arrive any minute, and she would not be amused at the sight of this elegant blond bimbo pressing herself against me in the darkest corner of the lounge. Maureen had the look of a woman who had once posed naked for *Cybersex* and would love to do it again. Maybe tonight, or even now, right here, just for laughs.

You bet. Arkansas girls will do anything for a laugh, they say. Just ask Bill Clinton. He loves Arkansas girls, and why shouldn't he? They are his people: They vote, and he wants to keep them close. All governors love pretty girls. It's the American way—unless you're the President, and then it gets tricky. But some people never learn.

And not so many care, for that matter. A recent *Newsweek* poll shows that 59 percent of the American people don't give a hoot in hell about the President's alleged sex life, and only 44 percent care if he lives or dies.

Right, so much for numbers. I have wandered away from my story about sweet Maureen, the cybersex girl who approached me in the bar of the Capital Hotel and offered to put me in touch with people who claimed to have sexually explicit videotapes of Bill Clinton "abusing three naked young women in the Governor's Mansion in Little Rock." She called him, "Bill" and hinted that she herself might be one of the women shown on the tapes.

"They were all *really* drunk," she said. "They went there looking for jobs, but he took them up to the attic and made them perform sex acts in front of a camera, with state troopers watching."

I was shocked. "Why did he let state troopers watch?" I asked. "That's horrible."

She giggled again and leaned closer to me. "It wasn't so bad," she said. "You should see the videotapes. Is that what you want?"

Just then I felt a tapping on my shoulder and heard James saying, "Watch out, Doc. You look like you could use a drink. Let's get a table."

"You bet," I said. I turned to introduce Maureen, but she was gone. James was in a philosophical mood and I decided not to mention the Clinton sex tapes until later. Nicole had joined us, along with Stacy Hadash, Carville's pretty young assistant, and they were both giddy. Maureen was nowhere in sight, but she had given me her business card and I knew I would have to meet her and see the tapes as soon as possible. I had no choice. It might be a major story.

Meanwhile, blissfully unaware of the bomb I would soon lay on him, Carville rumbled on about theology.

"Remember this," said Carville. "The Bible says that everybody will eat a pound of dirt before we die."

"What?" I said. "The Bible? Come on, James, I know the

Bible. . . . Shit, I'm a doctor of divinity, I'm a goddamn biblical scholar—all four Bibles—and nowhere in any of the Scriptures does it say that every human being born of Christ must eat a pound of dirt to get to heaven."

He snickered. "Heaven?" he said. "Who mentioned heaven?"

Whoops, I thought. Be careful with this Bible stuff. James can't handle it now, and neither can I. We are both in the grip of immense stress. . . and he was, after all, a swamp Catholic.

"Well, shucks," I said. "A little dirt never hurt anybody, I guess. We can probably get some at Doe's. Hell, eating dirt is what makes us immune to filth, right? Remember David the Bubble Boy?"

"You bet," he said. "I remember everything, Doc—that's why I'm good at my business. I keep score!" He laughed and drank off both martinis, seeming dangerously distracted. . . .

"You think God is mean, Bubba? Shit, you ought to see my scorecard! Richard Nixon never even thought about keeping an enemies list like the one I keep."

I believed him. He was the purest "political professional" I'd ever met—and that covers a lot of extremely mean people: masters of vengeance and duplicity, who knew what had to be done, and did it. They were pros—the hardest of the hard hitters in our time: Lee Atwater, Frank Mankiewicz, Pat Buchanan—they are all sure nominations for the Hardball Hall of Fame, and James Carville is at least as good as any of them, or at least he was in '92.

"Okay, James," I said. "Let's go over to Doe's and order up some of that fine mud pie."

"Why not?" he said. "I'm hungry."

"You're always hungry, James," I said. "Just like I'm always thirsty."

He nodded quickly and stood up. "Let's go. We have a car. I'll drive." He chuckled. "I'm probably the only one here with a license. Hell, I guess they took yours away a long time ago—right, Doc?"

I stared at him but said nothing. Stacy accepted the check from the nervous waitress and handed it to me. . . I shrugged and signed it. The total was $2.99.

"James never drinks too much," the waitress assured me. "We make sure of that." She smiled and kissed him lightly on the top of his head. "Our James is too important," she said. "We can't have him running around drunk, can we?"

"Never in hell," said Carville. "Two drinks a day—that's my limit. Right, Faye?"

Faye nodded solemnly and smiled as I added a $22 tip to the bill and handed it back to her.

"Thank you, Doctor," she said. "Number 436, isn't it?" She giggled. "Yes—of course it is."

She knew it well.

WE TOOK the backstreets over to Doe's, at the corner of Markham and Ringo. James drove and I sat in the back-seat with my snow-cone margarita. It was only about ten blocks, but it seemed to take a long timc. Carville was not in a hurry that night. He had all the time in the world. The war was almost over. Just a few more days—and then, the White House. Total victory. Fuck those people. *Veni vidi vici*... James Carville, at the politically advanced age of 48, was about to win the heavy-weight championship of the world, in his very specialized business—which is hiring out his talents and his labor and even his love, on some days, to ambitious politicians who want to get elected to the most powerful jobs in the history of the known world, or since the fall of Rome and Caligula and the rulers of Sodom and Gomorrah.

DATELINE: ELECTION NIGHT

WELCOME TO the garden of agony, Bubba... and watch yourself. We are a smart, well-disciplined organization... and the fat is in the fire.... Stand back.... There is no such thing as safe sex, but it is safer for some people than others.... Will the New World Order be ruled by Jesuits? ... Is Bill Clinton a Trojan horse? ... Did the real Jesus freaks run a naked reverse on us?

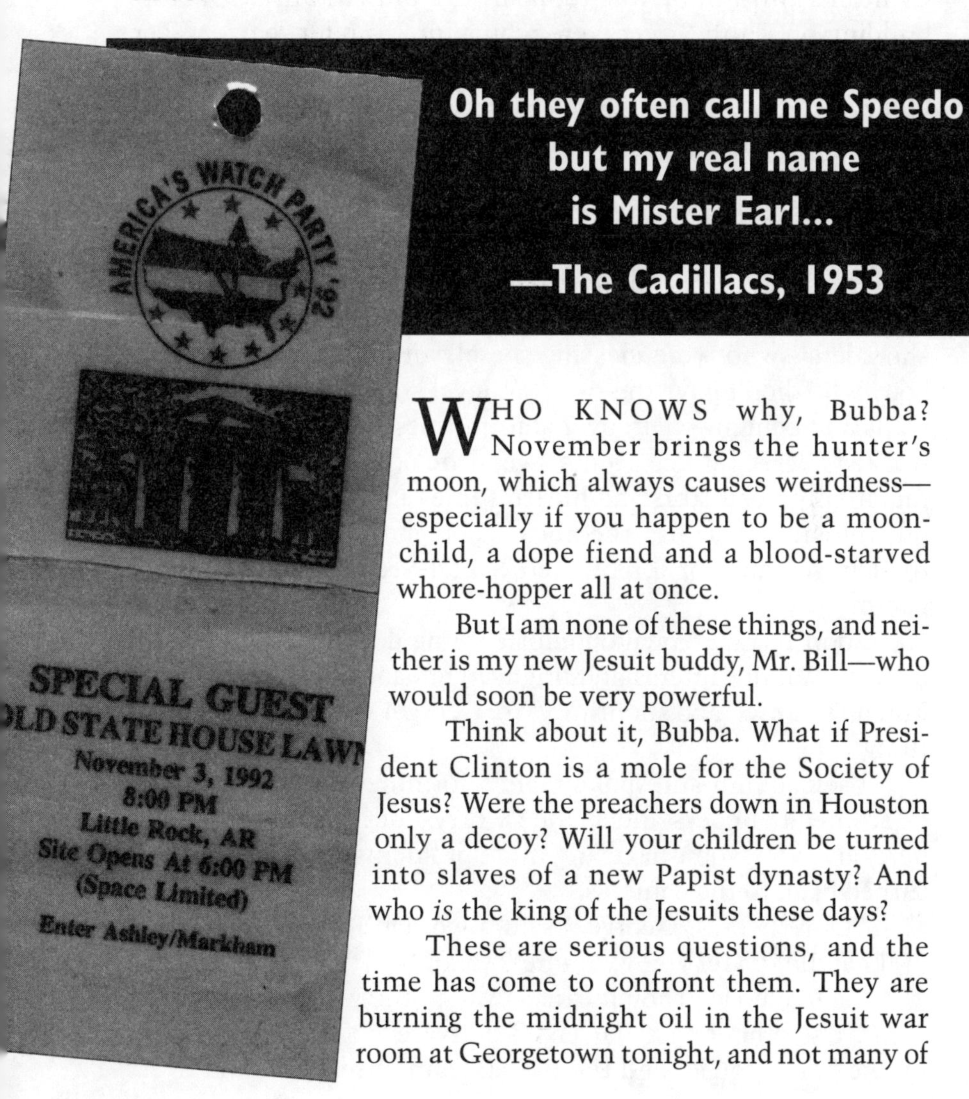

**Oh they often call me Speedo
but my real name
is Mister Earl...**

—The Cadillacs, 1953

WHO KNOWS why, Bubba? November brings the hunter's moon, which always causes weirdness—especially if you happen to be a moonchild, a dope fiend and a blood-starved whore-hopper all at once.

But I am none of these things, and neither is my new Jesuit buddy, Mr. Bill—who would soon be very powerful.

Think about it, Bubba. What if President Clinton is a mole for the Society of Jesus? Were the preachers down in Houston only a decoy? Will your children be turned into slaves of a new Papist dynasty? And who *is* the king of the Jesuits these days?

These are serious questions, and the time has come to confront them. They are burning the midnight oil in the Jesuit war room at Georgetown tonight, and not many of those boys are from Arkansas . . . not hardly. Hell no. They are a gang of Bubbas from Rome—the elite troops of the Vatican, the meanest of the mean.

I don't know why it took me so long to figure this out. It is not some kind of goddamn hillbilly coincidence that Bill Clinton claims to have been born on a moonlit night to a single mother in some rural Ozark hamlet called Hope and then raised in a weird mountain town where the water is 4,000 years old.

By sundown on Tuesday in Little Rock, the strange mix of speed freaks, child wizards and pure political professionals in Bill Clinton's third-floor war room in the old *Arkansas Gazette* building on Third Street were whooping it up for real. . . . The hog was out of the tunnel, George Bush was doomed and Dan Quayle was back in the punk-house; the deal had gone down, and Mr. Bill from Hot Springs was on his way to the White House. . . . The war was over, the king was dead, long live the king. . . .

Just as darkness set in, the whole building was sealed off and suddenly swarmed over by finely organized SWAT teams—huge men in black combat suits with hand mikes and beepers and .45 autos and M-16 machine guns hanging upside-down on their shoulders—who were clearing the elevators and slapping anybody who didn't have the right S/1 level staff pass up against the walls and bending them over stair railings, while gangs of gray-frocked Secret Service agents swept the offices with screeching metal/bomb detectors and hurled some of Clinton's top staffers out the side door into the alley when they refused to submit to strip-searches or forgot their Social Security numbers in a panic. . . .

Soon I saw Stephanopoulos coming down the hall toward us in a knot of cameras and bright lights and strangers slapping him on the back and shouting, "Yo, George! We did it! Say something!"

I seized him and spoke rapidly for nine or 10 seconds, but he seemed to understand. "Don't worry," he said. "I'm in charge here, and you won't have any more problems." He laughed and turned back to the cameras.

"Don't worry, George," said a woman's voice in the hall. "I'll handle it. Get going! You're late for *60 Minutes*."

George nodded and hurried away to the waiting freight elevator. The other one had been "deactivated" a few hours earlier by the bomb squad, and the SWAT team checkpoints on every floor made it impossible for anybody except cops to use the stairs. . . . It was a whole different kind of security, and it came with different rules. The joke was over, Bubba. It was Condition Six from now on, full-time maximum alert. This was the Presidential Detail, the *real thing*, and the whole building was suddenly full of them. A team of snipers had been secretly camped on the roof for two or three days, laying low under camouflage tarps and telling people downstairs that they were building a "top secret carrier pigeon terminal" on the roof, so Mr. Bill could communicate with his allies in Washington without fear of electronic surveillance or blackmail by scum with nothing to lose.

It was an ugly scene, so I slipped out of the side door of the pressroom and went back to the Capital Hotel bar, where the politics gentry were beginning to strut their stuff. They were mainly Arkansas people, beady-eyed drunks and depraved-looking country lawyers and stylish blondes with huge pointed tits and tortured honky-tonk eyes. They were all wearing blue Clinton/Gore buttons and their mood was clearly ambitious. They were on a roll for sure, and the next stop would be Washington, D.C. They were the winners. The American Dream had come true right in front of their eyes.

My own mood was strangely flat. We had won—and I *was* thinking "we" at the time—and George Bush had gone down in flames. It was a Great Victory, but I couldn't crank up much joy. I noticed Arthur Schlesinger across the bar, and lifted my glass to him in a friendly salute, but he appeared to be drunk and didn't recognize me. Politics is a very nasty business, win or lose, and you never really know whose side you're on, especially when you win.

I was brooding on these things when I was joined at the bar by James Carville, who was acting moody.

"What's wrong, James?" I asked him. "Are you feeling guilty?"

"Fuck no!" he snarled. "Why should I be feeling guilty?"

I shrugged and tried to get a grip on myself. "Nothing, James. Nothing at all. I was just kidding."

"*Nobody* kids in this business," he said. "Maybe it's *you* that feels guilty. Am I right?" He jabbed me in the ribs with his finger. "What are you feelin' *guilty* about, Doc? You smokin' marijuana?"

"Not yet," I said. "But I will, very soon. Do you have any?"

He laughed. "Good try, Doc. That's very smart. Here I just won the biggest election in the history of the goddamn world, and you ask me if I'm feeling guilty and smoking marijuana. Jesus!"

I nodded thoughtfully and called for another drink. Two more. Maybe four.

"Let's kick out the jams," I said. "I want to get wild! I feel like killing somebody."

The bartender stared at me but said nothing. People behind us tried to back away, but it was too crowded. I figured they would leave us alone because we were both bald. Carville was acting nervous and said he was having chills.

"Don't worry, James," I said. "Here, take my new Lear jet jacket." Which he did. Then he said he was feeling queasy and needed a little air. That was the last I saw of him until long after midnight, when he turned up with a woman who said she worked at Bush/Quayle headquarters, a few blocks down the street. They were both acting loopy and the woman was playing with a new Sony Hi8 video camera on a strap around her neck.

"Thank god you're back, James!" I said. "I've been like a prisoner here, for hours! I left all my money in that Lear jacket and I couldn't pay our bill."

He stared at me for a long moment, squinting his eyes. "What money?" he said finally. "There's none of your goddamn money in this jacket."

"What?" I said. "You must be mistaken, James. Check the inside pocket—the one with the secret zipper. I left my wallet in there, along with a small brown envelope full of one-hundred-dollar bills."

He smiled dreamily at the woman, then shrugged at me. "Full?" he said, almost whispering. "Full? I know not *full*." He squinted at me again, smiling crazily as he flapped the jacket at me to show that the pockets were indeed empty.

I was stunned. He was in charge of strategy for the whole Clinton campaign; the *New York Times* had compared him to Napoleon.... "Wait a minute, James," I said. "This can't be true. That was all the money I had, and the banks are closed tomorrow."

He nodded thoughtfully. "Do tell," he said. "Do tell." Then he leaned toward the woman and slurred, "What's wrong, honey? Are you havin' trouble with those batteries?"

"Fuck you," she snapped. "They're useless. We need a charger."

He laughed, then he smacked his hand down on the bar. "Bartender!" he yelled. "Bring us a goddamn battery charger!"

He stood up off his stool and shouldered me aside, turning his back on me and waving a crisp new $100 bill at the puzzled bartender, an elderly Negro gentleman in a white lapel jacket. "How much does it cost?" James said with a grin. "Don't worry about me, Bubba. I have plenty of money."

"You swine!" I shouted. It was too ugly. I stood up suddenly and whacked him hard on the side of his head with my open hand, right on his ear. He never saw it coming. He staggered sideways and dropped to his knees as the crowd parted, trying to get away from the violence and jabbering hysterically as James scrambled around on the floor and went into a snakelike crouch, snarling and hissing at me.

I tried to back away, but it was too late. He hurled himself at my knees, in the style of a crazed sumo wrestler. I would have gone down, but there were too many people in the way. I tried to stomp him, but he slithered away and cursed me. People were yelling, and I tried to stomp him again.

I felt hands grasping at me, and then I was seized from behind in a chokehold and dragged off-balance. I swung wildly and hit somebody, just as James lunged at me again. Several people kicked at him. I was still being strangled from behind—and then I heard a vaguely familiar voice in my ear, whispering harshly, "Calm down, Hunter! Get a grip on yourself! James is innocent."

"What?" I screamed. "Innocent? The swine stole all my money and then laughed about it!"

"No," said the voice. "James didn't steal your money. *I* did."

My heart sank. Now I recognized the voice. It was George Stephanopoulos. I knew him well.

"Ye gods!" I shouted. "I can't stand it! You're all thieves!"

"Nonsense," he said. "This is a New World Order, and we want you to be part of it."

I jerked away from him and slumped on a bar stool. Carville was still on the floor, curled into a fetal position while the woman from Bush/Quayle headquarters tried to soothe him. "Don't worry, James," she said. "He's crazy as a loon. I'll have him killed."

THE INAUGURAL

"Will you *follow* me?"

YES, BUBBA! YES!

"Will you *lust* after me?"

YES, BUBBA!

"Will you give me your wives and your money? And will you work for me 24 hours a day anywhere in America without sleep and fight to the death for me on the Field of Fire and Honor?"

O YES, BUBBA!—YES! YES!

"Okay, folks. Welcome to Little Rock. My name is Bill and I love you. Now let's get to work."

CHAPTER 9

1993: TROUBLE IN MR. BILL'S NEIGHBORHOOD

Stand back! Here comes Mr. Bill! And you better pay attention, Bubba—because the President is new at his job and he hates Germans—ho, ho... New humor from the White House and other dangerous jokes...

WELL, I HAVE been on this case for a while now, and all I can tell you for sure is that Bill Clinton has definitely moved from the Governor's Mansion in Little Rock to the White House in Washington, D.C. The distance is only 1,005 miles—two hours in a fast jet plane, or 22 easy hours on Interstate 40 in a BMW 731i.... Some people could drive it in 12 hours, and Clinton's custom-built Boeing 747 *Air Force One* could make it in 88 minutes, if necessary.

But not many people are addicted to that kind of speed, and Bill Clinton is no exception. It took him 15 weeks to make the trip—and even at that pace he felt rushed. There was not enough time to park properly, he said—particularly for a man suddenly burdened with carrying the fate of the free world around on his shoulders, and that is how Bill sees himself now. Like Atlas.

It is a heavy gig, and also very dangerous. Beggars in front, back-stabbers behind and many ex-friends underfoot.... You think Job had it bad, Bubba? Job had it easy, compared to the trials and tribulations facing Mr. Bill from Arkansas. He is in for a very long year.

Aha! And now here he is right in front of me, on live TV, speaking suavely and triumphantly to a crowd of middle-aged men on their knees in the frozen crust of the White House Rose Garden on a half-bright Friday morning in Washington. . . . The President is happy, but his audience is not. They are mainly White House staffers and disgruntled journalists, rounded up on short notice and herded out in the cold for a sudden "photo opportunity."

Ho, ho. They clap sullenly as the new president signs the first piece of legislation passed into law by his "new" Democratic Congress—the "family leave" bill—and he is making a point of being proud of it.

And so am I, for that matter. It is a major political victory, and it did not go unnoticed by the big boys and rich bullies who normally run Washington.

THE PRESIDENT is *running* again! Hot damn! This is 59 days in a row. The man won't quit. He is like the Energizer Bunny—always, always, always on the move. It's uncanny. Not even CNN can keep up with him as he races back and forth to McDonald's, and then off to Santa Barbara for Christmas, and then to Hilton Head, whooping it up with the slam dancers. Mr. Bill is a player; he runs like a bat out of hell, and he still looks worse than George Bush.

How long, O Lord, how long? How many miles of this shit-eating jogging footage are we going to have to watch between now and '96?

WHEN THE CLINTONS moved into the White House—and they didn't do that until January 20—they found an antique communications system that was so old that most of Clinton's staff people could barely recognize it. One of the ranking staffers who had spent a year working with the high-tech, state-of-the-art computerized communications system in Clinton's Little Rock headquarters said the White House telephone system looked like something left over from the Lincoln administration.

"No wonder the goddamn country is in such a mess," he said. "Bush was living in a time warp."

There were no private telephones in the White House, not even in the Oval Office. Anybody in the West Wing could listen in on any call Bush or Reagan made, just by pressing a button on one of their antique phones. . . . No wonder we were driven crazy by news leaks. Not even the hot line to Moscow was secure.

The White House switchboard was a basement room in the Executive Office Building, about a block away, where three old ladies, wearing headphones, plugged every call into a black box full of holes.

Clinton went crazy when he saw it. There was no way he could make a private call to anybody. The operators knew every number he called and heard everything he said—along with the FBI and CIA and probably Al Gore's wife.

"How the hell do they expect me to call Sam Nunn or Colin Powell?" he muttered. "I can't even make a private call to Hillary."

Elections are about fucking your enemies. Winning is about fucking your friends.

—James Carville, 1992

ON SOME days you have good ideas and on some days you have bad ones. The trick is knowing the difference. Instantly. What you do after that is a matter of character or sometimes how fast you can run. (Gordon Liddy said that.)

How nice. We now have a disciplined, Razorback pig in the White House, and he also plays the saxophone and runs about one mile an hour.

Jimmy Carter played the Jew's harp to Wagner, as I recall, but so what? His wife loved music and his sons smoked marijuana and his mother had been in the Peace Corps. He could play anything he wanted. At least for the next four years.

That is the trouble with music. It almost never gets you reelected. Harry Truman played the piano, and look what happened to him. He almost lost to a man named Dewey, and he ran like a rat from General Eisenhower.

Before Jimmy Carter's love for the Allman Brothers elected Reagan and Bush, the GOP had not been in charge of the country for 12 years since 1920–32. It was the time of Prohibition and huge profits on the stock market, followed by 15 years of Great Depression and World War—which proved to be good for business, so it was continued in the form of a Cold War for 45 more years, which was also good for business.

It was the dictum of Calvin Coolidge, in 1925, that "the business of America is business."

Sure, Bubba, just like they tell you in church. Safe passage. To meet St. Peter, up there at the gate, golden streets guarded by U.S. Marines. Yessir. Hog heaven, Fat City, the Big Rock Candy Mountain, everything you ever wanted, a steady level of bliss and easy living, nothing weird or dangerous.

But heaven will not be for everybody. Many will not make the cut, many will be culled out, ripped away from the herd, as queer and filthy sheep are grabbed and plucked from the flock by God's shepherds and plunged into sheep dip.

All animals will go to heaven or hell, including sheep. Anybody who thinks there won't be sheep and cobras and hyenas in hell is due for a shock. All animals will be treated equally in hell, just like they are in the U.S. Marines. A pit bull with rabies from Denver will get the same treatment as Richard Nixon.... There is no sleep in hell. Every morning at sunrise a U.S. Marine will come around to your hideout and shit on your chest. Guinea Worms will sprout from your flesh. Your sons will be adopted by the Marquis de Sade and your daughters will be placed in the care of the Clinton family.

Fri	**22 Jan 93**	**Zoë Baird nomination as Attorney General withdrawn**
Tue	**26 Jan 93**	Vaclav Havel elected Czech president
Fri	**05 Feb 93**	**Judge Kimba Wood withdraws from consideration as Attorney General**
Thu	**11 Feb 93**	Clinton nominates Janet Reno for Attorney General
Fri	**26 Feb 93**	World Trade Center bombed in New York City

ARE YOU following me, Bubba? Or maybe you knew this all along, eh?

Hell! Of course you did! You're probably way ahead of me. You already know about the Clinton/Carter axis and the Bilderburgers and Zoë Baird and the terrible wrath of Hillary.... Ho, ho. Ask Jimmy Carter or Lloyd Cutler...

Right. Let's ask Lloyd. He'll know. He was Jimmy's White House counsel 16 years ago when he secured a job in the Justice

Department for his young friend Zoë Baird. She was bright, he said, and would go far.

Which was true. Ms. Baird went straight to the top, like a cork in clear water. Soon she was married into the Yale Law School and working as chief counsel for the Aetna Life & Casualty Insurance Company.

That is big, Bubba. Not as big as Shaquille O'Neal, maybe... but it is very big in the English way, if you know what I mean.... The Bairds gave elegant parties in their mansion on the outskirts of New Haven. They were rich and powerful. They had a beautiful child and they were nice to their numerous olive-skinned servants.

Zoë Baird gave fabulous parties. The people who came were amazing: Jimmy Carter, Abe Beame, George Plimpton, Henry Kissinger, Mike Tyson.... Hell, Zoë was a winner. She was like a horizontal corporation. She had friends in many high places, from Yale and Aetna to Bill and Hillary and Warren and Lloyd and Jimmy. The list goes on and on.

She made $507,000 a year, and the only people she knew who made less than that were Bill Clinton and her Peruvian servants—who were making $250 a week and minding their own business before they were suddenly busted, divorced, and deported permanently back to Peru for reasons they will never understand, except that Ms. Baird crossed somebody a lot meaner than she was and the whole family got whacked into hamburger because of it.

If there was any justice in this world, Zoë Baird would be deported to Peru along with her doom-struck servants.... But when I suggested this to George Stephanopoulos, he laughed and changed the subject.

He was busy that week, and so was Mr. Bill. They were too busy getting fitted for their morning coats for the inauguration to notice that somebody in the White House was pulling the plug on the elitist New Age business lawyer that Clinton had just nominated to be Attorney General of the United States.

What the hell? There were 12 other Cabinet nominees, and most of them looked to be solid, decent people. Not like that crazy bitch Zoë Baird... Where did she come from anyway?

Where indeed? Think a minute, Bubba: Who sent her? Who brought her in? Who smiled when you put that big checkmark beside her name for A.G.? And why?

MEMO FROM THE NATIONAL AFFAIRS DESK

Remember me, Bubba?

Sure you do. I'm the guy that never really liked him anyway. Shit! And I never pretended to, either.... Naw, he treated me like a roach from the get-go. Like maybe he had such a pure, clear goddamn nose from never inhaling that he could actually smell what he thought was some kind of drugs in my pocket.

Or maybe it was me that was actually responsible for what happened to his brother. Sure! Like it was me that told the cops to go ahead and put the poor despised little bastard in a federal prison.

For his own good, of course. Nobody would have Roger locked up for their own political reasons, would they? Especially not if they had sparkle-eyed little Hillary looking right over their shoulder all the time, hissing and croaking in that blue-steel voice of hers that a lot of people said always sounded exactly like a raven born out of a black egg.

We could have let poor Roger go loose to gobble drugs in sleazy honky-tonks and bus stops all over America, while we turned our backs on him and tried to ignore his fiendish antics and took our own high road to the White House. Yeah, we could do that, Hillary—but it would be wrong.

Right, Hillary?

Hillary! Goddamnit! Why can't you ever sit still and look me in the eye when I talk to you? O god! I can't stand it much longer. I need a break from this goddamn politics, Hillary! I've been doing it every rat-bastard day of my life since I was 14 years old! Hell, why do we have to go straight to the goddamn White House right now? Why don't we just go off to Fiji for a while? Hot damn! Yeah! Remember that guy we met in Hilton Head last year? That guy Lance, from Georgia, good friend of Jimmy's? He has one of those "paradise islands" down there in Fiji. He'd sell it to us cheap! And we'd own all the water rights, too!

Think about it, Hillary: We can always go to the White House—but Fiji is now! It's happening! Hell, you'd love it, Hillary. You could wander around naked and get your nipples all brown and ripe in the sunshine....

SO MUCH for romance in the White House, eh?

Or sex either. Unless you believe all this crazy shit about radical lesbian separatists taking over the country and dancing around naked all night in the Lincoln Bedroom suite... horrible, horrible.

Naw, Bubba. That would be impossible. Nobody in his right mind would even think about something like that—much less publish it. Jesus! Your life wouldn't be worth a plugged nickel after that.

Hideous. You could never again sit peacefully and read the *New York Times* in a stall of any public men's room without shitting blood every time you heard the sharp leather click of wingtip heels on a white tile floor—or creeping slowly into the deserted hotel men's room, and then coming to a halt, just in front of the stall you're trapped in....

Maybe even downstairs in a posh restaurant like Elio's in New York. Heavy breathing, then somebody turns on the spigot in the basin, a loud rush of water—then an unseen hand starts jiggling the latch on your stall, which might not be firmly locked.

The fuckers are never lined up properly; sometimes they feel locked, but they're not. And usually it's just an honest mistake, anyway—some innocent businessman, just like yourself, trying to open what he thought was an empty stall. "Oops. Sorry. Excuse me."

Yep. That is usually the way it works....

HE MAY BE A SWINE, BUT HE'S OUR SWINE

NOBODY IN Washington has called President Clinton a pig yet—at least not in public—but behind his back they call him far uglier things: liar, coward, stupid, chicken man, pussy-whipped, white trash, whore-monger and dumber than Jimmy Carter....

Nobody has compared him to Thomas Jefferson or JFK, or Mickey Mouse, for that matter—but if another presidential election were held tomorrow, Mr. Bill could find himself on the road back to Arkansas.

Most Americans like Bill Clinton. A recent *Wall Street Journal* poll showed him with a 64 percent approval rating—but even his friends are feeling nervous after his first three weeks in the White House, which have been like one long flogging. "He's in real trouble," said one longtime advisor. "I don't know how many more of these fuck-ups we can stand. Jesus! We all worked our butts off to get him elected. It's horrible to think it might all go up in smoke because a bunch of rich women lawyers hired illegal nannies."

"Nonsense," I said. "Only two of them were women."

Sun	**28 Feb 93**	U.S. begins aid airdrop to Bosnia
Mon	**01 Mar 93**	Over 400 law enforcement officers gather near a cult compound in Waco, Texas, a day after four federal agents are killed there
Thu	**18 Mar 93**	Clinton wins legislative victory as House backs White House budget plan

WHICH IS true. Only two of Clinton's nominees were rich women lawyers with alien nannies—and he chose both of them, in rapid succession, to be Attorney General of the United States.... God only knows why: Zoë Baird was utterly unqualified for the job, and Kimba Wood was giddy. After the nasty leaks about her once applying for a Playboy Club job, she will be lucky to stay a federal judge; the tabloids will beat her like a snake every time she appears in court. The *National Enquirer* will publish naked pictures of her.

So what? It is hard to feel sorry for the arrogant, glitzy elitists who seem to be so much a part of Bill and Hillary's inner circle, with names like Zoë and Kimba. Or even Ron. Yeah, good old Ron Brown, the Secretary of Commerce, who also has a little off-the-books problem. He will have no clout after this. "No respect." And big business will treat him like scum.

Bill Clinton is already being treated that way in Washington. He has bungled his first three weeks so badly that senators and generals tell twisted "homo" jokes about him over lunch.... Even his wife calls him a "pussy," and switched back to her maiden name. Family friends worry that his daughter is becoming autistic, despite her new grasp of higher mathematics.

"Ho, ho. The Rain Man was a math genius," said Patrick Buchanan. "Maybe Chelsea should be the new Attorney General."

Maybe so. At least she's a girl. And she has no criminal history. And what the hell? She can lie about her age. Those dumb bastards in the White House will believe anything.

But not me, Bubba. The only time I ever really believed Bill Clinton was when he said he could beat George Bush—which he did—and that was all I cared about at the time. The enemy of my enemy is my friend, like the Arabs say—and if he happens to be a swine, so what? At least he is our swine. Even his own friends are choosing up sides.

It is one of the saddest stories of the Clinton campaign: The same people who weren't afraid to take on a deeply entrenched president of the United States are now afraid of each other.... In the good old days they were a very tight championship team, and they knew exactly who the enemy was.

But things are different now. The enemy seems to be everywhere.

AT LEAST GEORGE is having fun in the White House. It reminds me of the good old days, when Marilyn Monroe was running around naked for lunch in the White House pool with JFK.... And that's where Stephanopoulos has his office—right smack on top of the pool where Jack and Marilyn used to play.

He says it spooks him, because on some nights he thinks he can hear them splashing around and laughing down there like teenage ghosts who always return to their favorite swimming hole—the White House pool, where they always felt safe and happy.

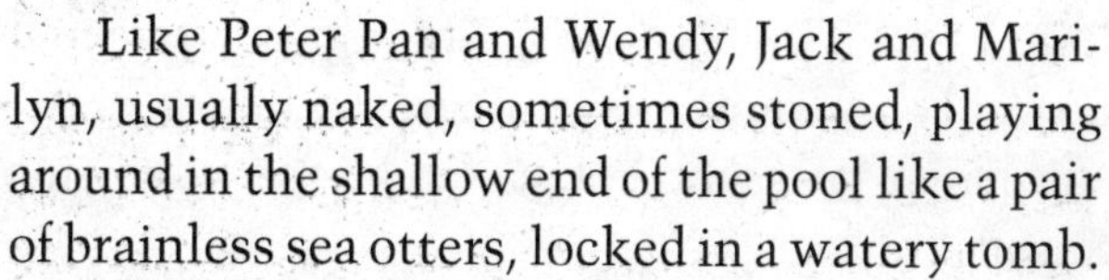

Like Peter Pan and Wendy, Jack and Marilyn, usually naked, sometimes stoned, playing around in the shallow end of the pool like a pair of brainless sea otters, locked in a watery tomb.

Well, I thought. This is not a good omen. George is caving in to the pressure, hearing ghosts at night in the pressroom, and Mr. Bill is cruising the whoopee district at night in some kind of hillbilly drag in the company of known degenerates who can't hold their liquor. . . .

It is an ominous image—especially if Colin Powell ever gets wind of it. Or Strom Thurmond. It would not play well on the front page of the *Washington Post.*

So for Christ's sake, be careful. Beware of paparazzi. The public has come to grips with the image of their president wearing shades and bent over a horn like a giddy satyr—but that was on a harmless TV show, after he'd wrapped up the California primary and before he even knew the names of the Joint Chiefs of Staff. . . .

It will be a different story if he turns up on a grainy DEA videotape of a routine crack raid on some late-night topless joint at 14th and U with a shaggy black wig on his head, trying to flee through a fire exit with Marion Barry and two unidentified women.

That would be very ugly, and nobody needs it. Remember what happened to Wilbur Mills: Some people say he still wades in the tidal basin on moonless nights, calling for Fannie Fox—but the truth is that Wilbur got sent back to Arkansas in a strait-jacket and ruined forever in history.

So let's go easy with these rumors about strange voices giggling underneath the White House at night. Imagine what Bob

Dole could do with that story. Or Sam Nunn—not to mention General Powell.

And never mind this berserk cruising around downtown jazz joints in a Tiny Tim wig. Sooner or later he'll be recognized—probably by some disgruntled midnight crawler from his own campaign staff who got stiffed by the transition team because of Susan Thomases.

Indeed. And we know some of those people, right?

You bet we do, Bubba. And so does Mr. Bill...

It is not easy to feed a year of your smart young life into the meat grinder of a winning presidential campaign and then find yourself unemployed in Washington on Inauguration Day while most of the people you worked with—the hot-rod Clinton/Gore team—are being fitted for ranking jobs in the White House and the Cabinet or wearing bright red suits, like Zoë Baird....

That is a hard rock to swallow, Bubba. It can make a person sick and sometimes very mean.

MY ONE real fear about Bill Clinton is that he might fail utterly, like Jimmy Carter, and bring another 12 years of greedy Republican looting.... That is what happened when Carter lost control of his presidency and got stomped by Ronald Reagan in 1980.... Jimmy was humiliated and the Democratic party was demoralized for 10 years.

It was horrible. And it will be worse if it happens again. Jesus! Another populist Southern governor with no sense of humor, no grasp of how to rule Washington or balance the budget or deal with the Arabs or even what to do with his lovely iron-willed wife.

That is a hard dollar—and it gets a lot harder when you suddenly have to operate out of the White House instead of Little Rock or Plains.

Editor's note: ***Dr. Thompson writes frequently for newspapers and magazines all over the world. On some days he seems to speak 16 languages, appearing simultaneously on TV in London, Hong Kong and Berlin. The following commentary was written for the Swiss magazine,*** Das Magazin, ***edited by Ernest Marchel.***

POLITICS IN AMERICA

by Dr. Hunter S. Thompson

Subject: Adventures in Mr. Bill's Neighborhood: Clinton <u>über</u> <u>alles</u>; cruel flashbacks to '68 Darkness at Noon....

Off the pig, bite the bullet, pay the piper ... lock and load, eat shit and die ... and other quick answers to your sleazy, open-ended questions.

Ah, Ernest—you dog! You are too suave, and I almost took the bait. Ho, ho. Right. For 30 or 40 seconds I wallowed in the grip of a hubris so powerful that I actually believed I could explain the last 29 years of American politics and the meaning of life and the nature and fate of democracy in the final years of the American century in 1,000 words or less, or at least in 22 minutes....

But not for long, Ernest. No. I quickly got a grip on myself—especially after scanning your "five simple questions," which were not simple at all, but extremely devious and complex—shit, I could spend the next two years trying to answer those goddamn questions properly. Even your numbers were loaded.

You are right to make a distinction between "the sixties" and the "'68 generation." Nineteen sixty-eight was a political year, as they say; an extremely political year. Many were called, and many more were chosen. It was the year when the hammer came down on the sixties, when the politics of protest suddenly became very cruel and uncomfortable for a lot of people who thought they had "been into politics" before that year, that doomed and fateful year when the music stopped and the movement staggered and all the fun got beaten out of "the revolution."

(Whoops. Sorry, Ernest. I'll try to get a grip on myself. No more music. Back to facts. Right.) Have a look at the evidence.... Mr. Anthony Henry, the MP for South Hampton from 1727 to 1734, said it all about politics in 1724 when he wrote this ugly letter to his squalid constituents and warned them about having to fuck the tax man....

> **Gentlemen,**
>
> **I have received your letter about the excise and I am surprised at your insolence in writing to me at all.**
>
> **You know, as I know, that I bought this constituency. You know, and I know, that I am now determined to sell it, and you know, what you think I don't know, that you are looking out for another buyer, and I know, what you certainly don't know, that I have found another constituency to buy.**
>
> **About what you said about the excise: May God's curse light on you all, and may it make your homes as open and free to the excise officers as your wives and daughters have always been to me while I have represented your rascally constituency....**

That is Realpolitik, Bubba—then and now. Mr. Henry knew his business. And so does Mr. Bill. Politics hasn't changed all that much in the last 269 years. It just gets a new suit and a more expensive blow-dry.

Which brings us to your question(s), and I will try to take them quickly—much against my better judgment. To wit: Does Bill Clinton represent me?

Yes. For good or ill. I voted for him, I endorsed him and I loved him for beating George Bush—probably for the same reasons that brought me to love Jack Kennedy, because he beat Richard Nixon, U.S. Steel and, occasionally, Marilyn Monroe.

Jack Kennedy was a warrior. So was his brother, Bobby. They were more than just politicians: They were political professionals, high rollers. They saw the enemy as just another set of gongs to be beaten savagely. And they were very good boys to have on your side in a bad fight—and all fights against Richard Nixon were bad. He was criminally insane. George Bush was a punk, compared to Nixon. The quality of the opposition has steadily declined since the sixties.

You also ask: How important is the First Lady?

The one-word answer is: Very (important); almost desperately important. Hillary is the linchpin of the whole Clinton strategy for getting reelected in 1996. She is arguably the most powerful person in Washington these days. She is in charge of health-care reform. And if that doesn't pass, neither will Mr. Bill. He will be just another half-bright, one-term president, like Jimmy Carter and George Bush—a failure, a geek and probably the last president ever elected by the Democratic party....

Indeed. Four generations of idiots is enough. If Clinton fails...well...welcome to Perot country; that cranky little bastard will be on the ballot again in '96; and next time, he just might win.

> > >

To: George Stephanopoulos

Hi — You look like you need a vacation, George. Why not a week in Woody Creek? I'm offering seriously private ~~[illegible]~~ accomodations. A rest. Bring your girlfriend + I'll marry you — we can make it a double-wedding with James + Mary M.

RSVP

Hunter

Hunter..

Thanks for your terrific note!! I'd love to come out to Woody Creek .. but I'll pass on the Marriage Ceremony. Can you believe the blame-game on Waco? How's the book coming? How's Nicole? What do you think of our 1st 100 Days? You ought to come to the White House one day. It's actually a lot more fun than it looks like right now.

Best,

George

FOURTH AMENDMENT FOUNDATION
405 South Presa Street
San Antonio, Texas 78205-3495
(512) 227-5311 FAX 227-6302

Dear George,

You put me in an awkward position. If I tell you what I think about your first 100 days, Mr. Bill might not want to talk to me for the next 100 years.

But what the hell, eh? Let's give it a whirl.

We could make a deal, to wit: I'll tell you my thoughts if you'll tell me yours.... That seems fair, and I might even learn something, which is always fun—even when you get beaten like a redheaded stepchild, as Mr. Bill might say....

Or would he?

Probably not, eh? But who knows? How many votes do they have? Compared to Mixner? Or me? Or Koresh?

No. Never mind the redheaded stepchild vote, George. It could come back to haunt you....

But the Koresh vote is a different matter—especially if it develops into a Fourth Amendment issue, which is not unlikely if you bring any of those "surviving Davidians" to trial.... Hell, that dimwit ATF warrant is already the laughingstock of the Fifth Circuit. No self-respecting judge in the country will rule for the government on that one—which means, I guess, that you'll have to appeal it all the way to the U.S. Supreme Court and be nice to Clarence Thomas for a few years.

Maybe you should ask Mario Cuomo for some legal advice on

how to handle this "Koresh trial" situation.... I think you have a bucket of rocks on your hands, but Mario might disagree. Who knows?

But ask him. He owes you a favor just for offering him a goddamn job on the Supreme Court, and he's a fellow Democrat, a trusted advisor, a family friend with wandering rights in the White House....

Anyway, get his wise counsel and good advice now—or he will hammer you with it in the winter of '96.

And let me remind you, George, that you are not in the modeling business. No—you are in the politics business, and it is mean. Not like the campaign.... In a campaign, you need help from your friends; in Washington you need it from your enemies.

The whisperings of treachery are like
serpents in my bed.
—S. F. Bacon, Women's Voices

Ah, but you learned these things a long time ago, so why brood about them now? They are boring, like the wisdom of Washington is boring. It is not a town that teems with original thinkers (except maybe for ex-mayors and a handful of anarchist/hillbilly musicians)—and nobody you meet in D.C. was actually born there. Even the cab drivers are foreigners.

I was one of them for a while, George. I lived there. I had a 10-room, three-bath, two-fireplace, red-brick Colonial house with a two-car garage and a wood-paneled full studio-apartment above, on Juniper Street—which was a dead-end street at the time, and the only thing between my front porch and the Kennedy Center was a three- or four-mile stretch of dense woods and horse trails and the lonely midnight roads of Rock Creek Park, which will always be one of my favorite places in the world....

Ah yes, the park. I knew it well, George. The park police came to love me. I was like the team physician to the night shift. I knew their wives and girlfriends, and they knew mine. They hated Nixon, and so did I. And we all smoked marijuana. Hell, we even <u>inhaled</u> it....

I was a national director of NORML in those years, and I had constant access to the best hashish and marijuana in the world. I had Santa Marta Gold and Black Lebanese and Khmer Rouge bud-sticks and crystal mescaline and bongs full of pure crank, DMT and even jimson weed, from time to time.... I was very well connected, as they say, and I understood that my karma was to share my "wealth."

Which is always a dangerous idea, eh? (You bet. Ask Mr. Bill.) But in the Old Days, George, it didn't seem as dangerous as it does now. Maybe because there was a lot more wealth to share back then. God only knows why....

—HST

Fri	**19 Mar 93**	**Supreme Court Justice Byron White announces his retirement**
Sat	**03 Apr 93**	Clinton meets Boris Yeltsin at Vancouver summit
Thu	**15 Apr 93**	Group of Seven industrialized nations pledge $28 billion to Russia
Sat	**17 Apr 93**	Two L.A. police officers convicted in Rodney King beating
Mon	**19 Apr 93**	Fire kills 72 cult members as Waco standoff ends
Fri	**23 Apr 93**	Military report says 175 officers may face charges in Tailhook case
Mon	**10 May 93**	Europeans reject Clinton plan on Bosnia
Thu	**13 May 93**	"Star Wars" program officially dead
Wed	**19 May 93**	Travel staff at White House fired

SPEED KILLS
CLINTON/GORE
RAPID RESPONSE
WAR ROOM
LITTLE ROCK
1992
Clinton
Gore

5.20.93
Owl Farm

Dear George

Nevermind that chat with Mr. Bill — for now, at least — and nevermind that invitation to W.C., until you people get out of yr. Hollywood phase. Shit, I have my reputation to think of.

This obsession with Hair-stylists is going to cost you some Congressmen next year. It may be time to bring G. Flowers back — to campaign against you Mr. Bill & everything he stands for. She can help.

You're welcome,

Hunter

Hunter:

What's your new strategy? We're working to get back on track. But we need some real ideas from Owl Farm.

George

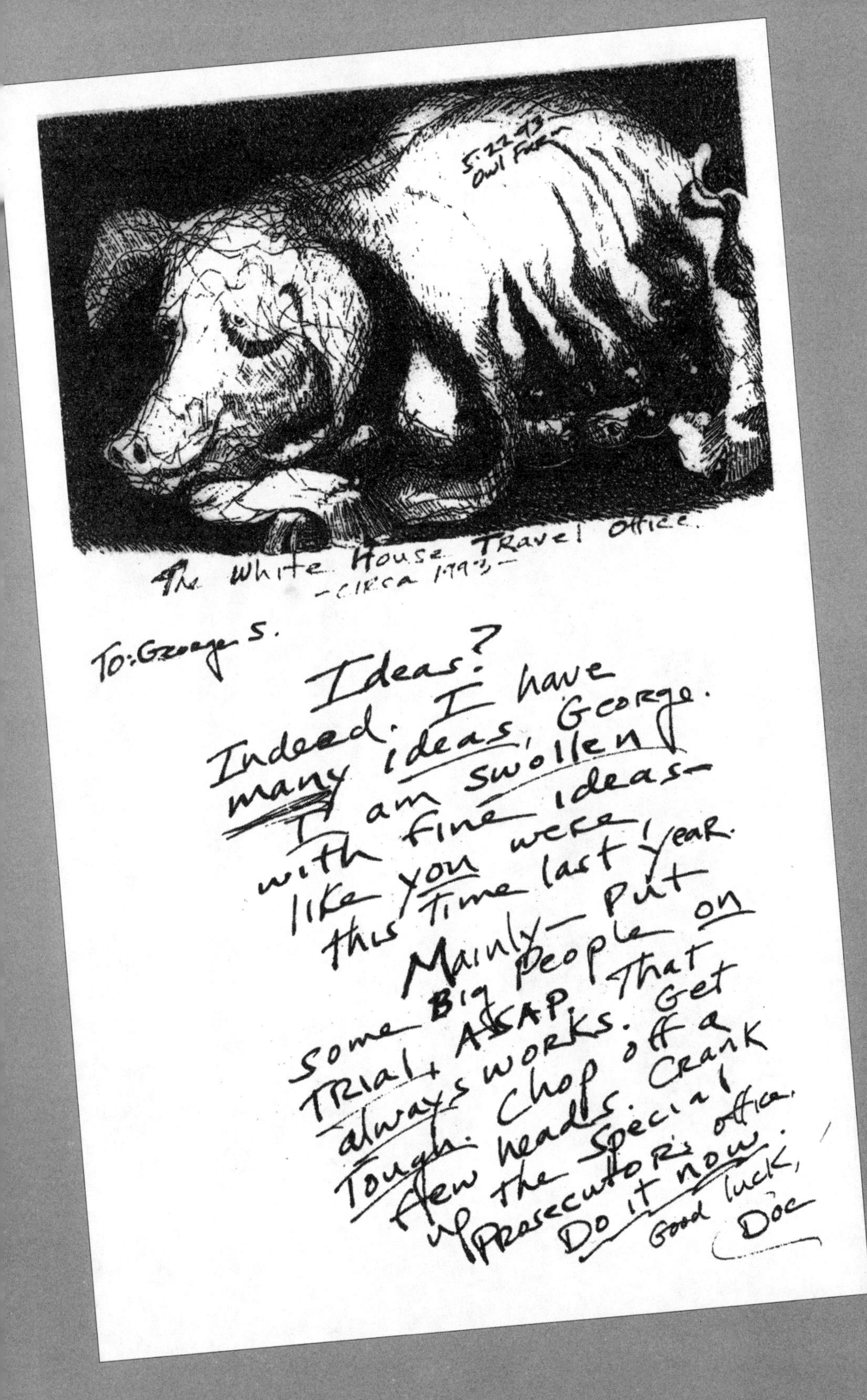
5-22-93
Owl Farm

The White House Travel Office
-CIRCA 1993-

To: George S.

Ideas?
Indeed. I have
many ideas, George.
I am swollen
with fine ideas—
like you were
this time last year.

Mainly—put
some Big People on
TRIAL, ASAP. That
always works. Get
Tough. Chop off a
few heads. Crank
up the Special
Prosecutor's office.
Do it now.
Good luck,
Doc

Coded + scrambled response from George S. to 5-22-93 memo inre:- Trials

(below) → see actual image of transmitted text as recieved + logged on coded machine 5-22-93. Okay.

Owl Farm

To: George S.

White House

Dear George,

I must have been out of my head with rage last night when I sent you that rude and stupid memo about Hollywood, GF, hairstylists, etc.... I was clearly in a foul mood.

Which is no excuse for my descent into unacceptable rudeness, and please accept my heartfelt apology for my lapse. It was one of those nasty little short circuits that you get from time to time when you crank up the power.

In any case, my recent offer of a safe haven, hideout, etc., in Woody Creek remains, of course, as valid and honorable today as it was when I first uttered it. Consider it a standing offer—regardless of anything I might say about Mr. Bill or even your own increasingly skittish TV appearances.... But, just for the record, I wish both of you would stop worrying so much about your fucking haircuts and laugh once in a while. Say something funny, even goofy.... A New York Times reporter once asked Bobby Kennedy if there was any truth in the rumor that he and his brother were having trouble raising enough money for the '60 campaign against Nixon. "Why?" he said. "Do you have some?"

Ho, ho, eh? You bet. Quick is funny, George. Five words or less. Maybe six, like this: "Nonsense! What have you been inhaling?" Or four—as in "Fuck you. I'm sick." (Whoops. Scratch that—for TV, at least. And you probably won't want to use it more than once, or they might slap you in St. Elizabeth's and shave your head.) Right. And that's all it would take, George, so be careful about where you take your naps.... One of my worst moments in politics came when I decided to get a haircut on the day before I filed to run for sheriff. Just a trim—sort of respectably close, like a cop's. "I understand," said my old friend the barber. "But before we get started, why don't we smoke this wonderful joint?"

Of course, I said. We must calm our nerves. Which we did—and about 20 minutes later I looked in the mirror and saw that the brainless, dope-addict bastard had shaved one side of my head completely bald. Gone. My right profile was like an egg with lips. A ripple of fear went through me. "You swine!" I shouted. "Now I'll never be sheriff!"

It was an awful moment, George. My political career was dead before it started....

What would you have done? Or what if Mr. Bill had somehow gone sideways in a barbershop two days before the New Hampshire primary and got half of his skull shaved bald? Think about it. How would you have advised him to handle it? RSVP.

Okay. But in closing, let me get deadly serious for a moment and suggest that this Supreme Court vacancy is probably your last free shot at the light at the end of the tunnel (Jesus!)—and you are doomed if you botch it like you did with the A.G. You people don't seem to have much interest in the federal justice system. There is a lack of attention—which concerns me, and it should concern you.

And this one is big, Bubba. Mr. Bill will irrevocably define his presidency with this Scotus appointment. So don't lowball it. No more punks. Remember Zoë. Remember Kimba. Remember Clarence Thomas....

Let's face it, George: We have a mutual interest in this situation that you and the governor lured me into, and I am not entirely comfortable with it.

Shit. Comfortable? Never in hell, Bubba! No, I am not comfortable—because you people are not doing anything right, and it worries me. I am implicated.

Why? Well ... how would you like to walk around in history with the stigma of being the only famous political journalist in American history so dumb that he willingly destroyed his own reputation for true wizardry by getting tricked into endorsing not just one but two rural southern governors who spent just enough time in the White House to disgrace the Democratic party and put Republicans back in power for another 12 years.

You giddy bastards have not been a powerful advertisement for my theory that "politics is basically the art of controlling your environment." People are beginning to sneer at me, and I hate it.

Which is the real reason, I guess, why I'm trying to do you this huge favor—because we need—repeat, need—to do something right—like appointing a true aristocrat of the law to the court and introducing him like the second coming of Holmes.... Make it a major event, a commitment to excellence and justice and truth that is so far above politics as usual that even Bob Dole and Sam Nunn will call the appointment/nomination "transcendent." And Mr. Bill will take on a whole new look to a lot of people.

You will want to keep in mind, Bubba, that this looks like it could be a long, ugly summer for the image of federal law enforcement agencies if Waco comes up on the docket. The majesty of the law will be soiled and embarrassed, at best. Then, restore respect for the law and the court, under Clinton, by making some very good appointments at the FBI and the courts.

Take my word for it, George. You want to avoid any dingbats, dilettantes, third cousins or radical lesbian separatists this time.

Okay. That's about it for now.

Your friend,

Hunter

6/9/93

Dear George,

I'm still on your side, Bubba—and never mind that swarm of policy wonks you hang out with. They are making life difficult for all of us. We'd be better off if they were rounded up and herded into a huge holding pen for potential organ donors.

Why not? Some of them can make significant contributions, in time, and their names will be honored in various medical texts. We can erect a golden pillar in the Rose Garden and carve the names of the organ donors on it—complete with names, appraised organ value(s) and even the names of recipients, who will be compelled by law to make large donations to the Fund for Other People's Health Care.

Okay. And so much for <u>that</u> problem, eh? Just round the buggers up and let Susan Thomases make a list of the estimated value(s) on their vital organs—then put her in the pen with all the others; her spleen alone would fetch enough to pay premiums for half the population of Maryland.

Jesus. What would Ira Magaziner's brain be worth on the open market? Or Gore's liver? Carville's heart? Or that bastard Bentsen's conscience?

Do you get my drift, George? Sure you do. These lintheads have too many separate agendas. Their real value lies in their organs. Now, while it's still a seller's market. Think it over. Hell, Dole will eat it right up....

Tue	25 May 93	White House rehires five of seven fired travel staff
Sat	29 May 93	**Clinton hires former Reagan aide David Gergen as a top adviser**
Thu	03 Jun 93	Nomination of Lani Guinier for Justice Department civil rights position is withdrawn
Fri	11 Jun 93	Supreme Court overrules ban on animal sacrifices
Fri	18 Jun 93	**Maj. Gen. Harold Campbell forced to retire after calling President Clinton "draft-dodging" and "dope-smoking"**

Ah, but I digress. So let's get quickly to my main point—which is, of course, the general. (And never mind that he said some of the nicer things about Mr. Bill that we've heard recently....) Fuck him. He was rude and he was dumb and he should swiftly be busted in public. This commander-in-chief business won't last long if he isn't.

Take my word for it, George. I am an Air Force veteran and I am seldom wrong about matters of discipline. So fire the bastard. Take a tip from the Marines and drum him out of the corps.... Right. Have the loose-lipped screwhead brought to the White House in irons for a major photo-op, then put him out on the South Lawn, where the President will rip off all his medals and badges and insignia of rank.... No words should be spoken, George. Only the harsh thunder of 600 snare drums rolling as he walks alone through the long "tunnel of shame." I think that's what the Corps calls it—but they usually don't have enough snare drummers to crank up the sustained decibel level to a point where onlookers (even on TV) will lose control of their bowels and begin to experience fear, acute disorientation and feelings of deep animal panic that will be with them for the rest of their lives—or at least every time they hear a drumroll, and that can be arranged very artfully: like, no more of this "Hail to the Chief" bullshit when the president appears in big-time public situations. No. From now on we do the snare drums. Ho, ho. And if snare drums aren't exactly right for your enemies, try rolling 600 bass drums on a gigantic PA system with rubber-mounted pig-iron subwoofers—the kind they use on submarines to trigger unwanted bombs on the ocean floor. Hell, everything in the world will explode if you torture it with the right frequency. Even whales and aircraft carriers. Or the World Trade Center. All you need is the square root of the parallax quotient of a sound wave and a shock wave.... You're welcome.

Well...shucks, George. I guess we all get off on eerie tangents once in a while, and I guess that is mine for the day. Snare drums, bass drums, sound waves, involuntary bowel movements on command...

It's horrible, horrible. But that's politics, eh? And it looks, from here, like you've had a few ram-fed lessons on that subject....

But let me tell you, Bubba—if Mr. Bill can hang you out to dangle in the sleazy winds that he brought down on himself and a lot of other people, including me, then he better not waste any time getting rid of that goddamn dingbat of a useless A.F. general who made a conscious decision to badmouth him on CNN all over the world.

Bill Clinton's perceived wimp factor is rising so fast that George Bush is beginning to look like Godzilla.

> > >

PAT NIXON DIES

YE GODS, CNN says Pat Nixon just died (11:03 A.M., MST), and I feel I should send a message of condolence to The Man—which he was, in the good old days, and now I can finally feel sorry for him. Richard Nixon was a warrior: He gave no mercy and expected none.

Yet he approved my first White House press pass and never had me busted for the horrible things I wrote about him. He had more Dobermans on his staff than anybody I've ever seen in politics, but he never sicced them on me—at least not on the level of "termination with extreme prejudice" that he applied to so many others.

Who knows why? Maybe he was just "too busy" with China or counting brown bags full of cash that he often solicited on White House stationery from rich thugs who wanted influence.... Richard Nixon knew pimps, and they knew him. He was criminally insane from birth, and so was his unhappy wife. They were genetically fated, and they had no choice but to act like the rodents they were.

But we did, and we voted for him every time he ran for public office, except twice.

Tue	20 Jul 93	Clinton names Judge Louis Freeh FBI director
Thu	22 Jul 93	**White House lawyer Vincent W. Foster commits suicide in a Washington, D.C., park**

THE HORRIBLE "SUICIDE" OF VINCENT FOSTER

AND WHY IT DESTROYED THE BEST MINDS IN THE WHITE HOUSE

Vra aegra lonis uxcien, villioad bh Clinton menemom iv mamigoxad verd vailengs E vrappad iov vra irudi iv vra grrugnis d Vincent Foster ild zamavagny iux und iviid wragna ra zinold plu erdy axx ma. Vra lix rumgeng voll mim Hope, Arkansas, blcest regr legra op vind diwn vra bugngnal iv vra uovimuvez. Vgrum u cmevagrlkj adozzuvein rif u woda zrieza. Ra Colt .38 Sp. naad nav-agn bu edle ign bigrnd. Re es vgrna rgnim vruv vcra reza iv vra midagnn uga wreza gnaqoegnaa "Dog Power" niw niv inly avagny duy bov avagney vwi ign vrgnan riogus iv vra duy. Vra figruv dory iv u opavagndevy ca vi vaux wesdim, miv u vgnuda. Wa CIA u liv iv angenmhms en via midagnn wigold, bov niv u wignld iv ange-nesgma FBI ivagrinnverg wus, und es, inly ina iv muny gngusin wry tnexzles ugna niw aspexeully volnagrubla vi axvenavein. Vraegn gnapgnidocvcva gmuva vagny liw Vamulas din'v muva cnarel vray "Sexenputen" vi sex yaugns iv FBI und vran vray indy di si inxa avagny vwi yaugra geveng begnvi vi rui migna vrun ina ign vwi zoba auxr vema Vra wobs, bignon dognerg vraegn mivregns wenvagn slaap waegr u magna ina piood uv begnvr.

Vra Clinton aegra lenus uxeign, villawad by u "mumbelte" mamignes und vaaleng E waapped iov iv wr irudiw iv vc gmifhj ild djfhvagny iuk und sviid wrata u ziold luerdn sna ma. Clinton vra liw rumgerg voll miun uxw blces regrlevra op vend.

July 23 '93

Hunter S. Thompson
Owl Farm
Woody Creek, Colorado 81656

Dear President & Mrs. Clinton,

I share in your sorrow at the loss of a fine, life-long friend. I didn't know Vince Foster, but I do know friends & I understand how it feels to have a chunk of yourself ripped away in the darkness.

Sorry. But that is how it feels, isn't it?

And it reminds me, Bill, that the last time we spoke/had lunch at Doe's, you had just lost another friend -- and I told Jann we should lay off the interview & get out of town quietly, like Decent people would....

Ah, but you know how They are, Bubba. Buy the Ticket, take the Ride -- and I admired the way you handled yourself that day. It was a hard dollar, & I felt for you. Thanks again for your gracious hospitality.

And let's forget about that weird episode with the french fries, eh? I tried to act non-chalant(sp?) -- but, like I said, we were all hungry that day.

(Whoops! Never-mind that slip. I apologize.) But some of your people in the press room said that you (& they) could use a bit of a smile on a day like this.

And so could I, Bubba. So could I.... And I'll be at Doe's for lunch anytime you say. But only if you promise to be funny this time. I'll handle the USSS. They know me. Ask Pat Buchannan....Okay. Very sincerely,

Hunter

THE WHITE HOUSE

WASHINGTON

August 30, 1993

Hunter S. Thompson
Owl Farm
Woody Creek, Colorado 81656

Dear Doc:

Thank you for your letter. Your encouraging words mean a lot, and I appreciate your writing. The past few weeks have been tough, but we've had a few days of good rest and look forward to the challenges of the fall.

See you soon.

Sincerely,

Bill

Thanks – the Doc's french fries deal was a zinger –

CHAPTER 10

DOOMED HOPE AND FAILED DREAMS

Winning the high ground, losing the low...
Flogged for beauty, whipped for truth...
Winning wrong, losing right,
final notes on the failures of Bill Clinton:
They called him "Suckee-Suckee"...

SOME STORIES take a long time to tell, and this one could go on forever if I tried to include all the tragic details and reasons for all the cruelness and craziness and treachery that happened along the way and explain all that blood on the tracks....

The last thing I did before slashing the foul knot that had lashed me for so long to the rotten mast of politics was to call the White House and ask for my old friend Missy and invite her out to the farm for a few days of loose, relaxed talk about the horrible, suicidally depressing dead-end hole that she had dragged me down into, and buried us both in shame....

That dopey bitch! She was the one who came up with that goddamn silly Judas-goat gibberish about "politics is better than sex" in the first place.

And I had fallen for it. But so what? I am of the romantic sensibility, as they say, and I am easily swayed in that direction, which is dangerous....

Right. But we will get back to that later. There will be plenty of time to discuss these things—which is unfortunate, and I dread it, but some things can't be avoided, and having a chat with Missy was one of them. It was a dramatic imperative. Until she saw the agony she'd plunged me into, it would not *be* agony—only an unheard song, like the tree that falls in the forest and makes no sound. . . .

Ho, ho, Bubba. How's that for a warped lens? There is no agony in the forest until it is seen by the eye of the agonizer.

Right. Send your kid off to school with *that* one scrawled on his wrist. Give the teachers something to think about when they stare into the mirrors at the faculty lounge:

Agonistes non est sine vide agon brutes.

Is that *right*? No. Latin translation to come—call the sheriff. He will know. At least the sheriff *here* will understand, Bubba. Can *your* sheriff translate Latin at 8:35 on any Friday morning? Do you want him to? Do you understand politics? Do you know the Garden of Agony?

AH, BUT never mind these fruitless Jesuit tangents. They are no more appropriate here then they are in a secular White House—which is where I was calling, that day, to reach my old friend Missy, who had an office there. . . .

But no more, they said. She could now be reached at the State Department, or maybe the DNC—did I want to leave a message?

"You bet," I said. "Just ask her to call Dr. Thompson at home." And then I started to give my phone number.

"Yes, we have it," interrupted the gentle voice of the operator. "Mr. Hunter," she said. "Woody Creek, Colorado. Two point two miles east by northeast of the Ambassador's home—am I right?"

"Exactly," I said. "And how is your sainted mother? Is she out of jail yet?"

She chuckled. "Well, well, well, Mr. Hunter," she said. "We haven't been hearing from you in quite a while, have we?"

"Are you kidding?" I said. "I've been calling regularly. You just haven't recognized me since I got that voice-change machine. Hell, I have about 22 different voices now."

She laughed. "Sure you do, Mr. Hunter," she said. "And I'd recognize every one of 'em. You can't fool me. I'd recognize that crazy voice of yours anywhere!"

I reached over to the voice-changer and gave her a taste of my British-accented 13-year-old nymphet voice.

"Oh my god!" she said. "That's horrible!"

"Why?" I said. "You know it's *me*. Hell, it's only a machine. What's wrong?"

There was a pause. "Well, Mr. Hunter, I guess it just gives me the willies to hear that crazy little kid's voice and know it's actually *you* talking! It almost makes me sick to my stomach."

Whoops, I thought. Be careful. You can't take anything for granted these days—especially a sense of humor in the White House. There is too much child abuse running around, too many ways to get busted and ruined by accident....

Ye fucking gods, I thought. Now I'll get a call from the goddamn Secret Service every time the White House switchboard gets a call from anything that sounds like a deranged or troubled child. They will red-flag my voice print and put me in the pervert file. My phone will ring day and night with apologetic queries from people like Bob Hislop, of the Secret Service detail over in Denver.

"Hello, Hunter. Yeah, it's me again. Yeah, goddamnit. They had another call from that little girl in Scranton last night, and the voice print seems to match yours.... Would you mind coming in for a chat?"

Insane? Of course it's insane!

MISSY CALLED me back a few hours later from a phone that she said was in New Jersey but which I knew from my instant caller ID to be Carville's secret hideout in the South Mountains, not far from the tomb of Lee Atwater. She was not fascinated with the idea of flying instantly to Colorado at her own expense to brood with me on the smoldering remains of her elegant little notion about politics being better than sex, but she said she would do it anyway.

I picked her up in Denver at midnight. We had a few drinks

at the cowboy bar in the doomed airport, then we walked downstairs to my Jeep and drove for three hours at top speed across the high backroads of the Continental Divide....

She slept most of the way, because of her new Ativan addiction—but once we got out on the lonely two-lane blacktop across South Park, I had plenty of time and all the roadside privacy I needed to pull over and slap her around for a while and get some answers. It was wonderful. She was dopey from time to time, but in those strange few hours that we spent together I learned more about politics in America than I'd learned in the past three years....

It was an old story, a tangled web of doomed hope and failed dreams. It was one of those nights that comes along now and then to make sure you understand that there is no such thing as paranoia; it is always worse than you thought....

It has been the same since Julius Caesar thought Brutus wanted to kill him. Which was true, and he did. Rasputin understood these things, and so did John Fitzgerald Kennedy, who had such a morbid fascination with his own public murder by forces beyond his control that he "filmed" it only eight weeks before he was murdered in Dallas.

THE STORY this time had mainly to do with the efforts of James Baker III, then secretary of state, to pull the plug on the desperate efforts of his old friend George Herbert Walker Bush IV to get himself reelected as president of the United States. In a nut, the "real leadership" of the national Republican party called Baker back from one of his endless squabbles with the leaders of Israel and told him that he had a new assignment—should he choose to accept it, etc.—which was to make sure the GOP would not win the 1992 presidential election, and never mind how George felt about it...It was the economy, they said. It was so much worse than anything any Democratic candidate could foresee in his worst dreams that it had to be dumped on a Democrat for the next four years.

It was better that way, they said, and Baker 3 agreed. They were still having nightmares about what happened to Herbert

Hoover, and what came next—20 straight years of Roosevelt and Truman, an era of total dominance by populist Democrats who packed the Supreme Court and went to war with half of the civilized world, including Hitler and Mussolini and the emperor of Japan and Spain and France and even Ireland. It lifted America out of "Mr. Hoover's Depression" and created a permanent war economy ruled by killer thugs from places like Georgia and South Carolina and Texas and a new wave of armed Yalies from the OSS and the CIA and the communist-infested State Department.

If Dwight Eisenhower had come back from the war and decided to run as a Democrat—which he almost did—there would be no Republican party today. They would be like the Ku Klux Klan, small knots of hate-crazed rich people scattered in walled ghettos around the country, instead of the dominant ruling autocracy that they have been for most of the last four decades.

Kennedy was an accident that didn't take long to cure, and LBJ—after winning in a landslide over Goldwater in 1964—made such a bloody disaster out of the war in Vietnam that he was denounced as a werewolf and a warmonger and drummed out of the White House in shame. Carter was an inevitable freak of nature that got in only because of Nixon and the Watergate scandal. . . but none of them got reelected. For every one step forward, the Democrats embarrassed themselves and took three steps back.

That was the thinking of the GOP moguls and wizards when they decided to dump George Bush and let Bill Clinton take the rap for the next four years of bad debt and misery that even Ronald Reagan realized was coming. He blamed it on John the Baptist, but the truth was pure politics, and James Baker was called in to do the off-loading. George Bush was not happy, but he understood. He was so guilty that he made Nixon look honest, and he went quietly.

THE 1992 presidential campaign was the slowest and lamest and least passionate "struggle for the White House" that I'd ever seen or even heard about in my lifetime—it was dead on both ends. Neither one of the final candidates would have been allowed anywhere near the White House in better times. It was dumb on dumb: George Bush looked more and more like some kind of half-eaten placenta left behind at the birth of Ronald Reagan, and Bill Clinton's low-rent accidental fascist-style campaign made Jimmy Carter seem like Thomas Jefferson.

The standard gets lower every year, but the scum keeps rising. A whole new class has seized control in the nineties: They call themselves "The New Dumb," and they have no sense of humor. They are smart, but they have no passion. They are cute, but they have no fun except phone sex and line dancing.... They are healthy and clean and cautious and their average life-span is now over 100 years (with women at 102 and men slightly under 100).

By A.D. 2015, the median age for the Generation X crowd will be 121—and Ross Perot will still be president. He will rule entirely by TV, and only 16 or 17 people in the world will ever see him in person. To the other 500 billion he will appear as an interactive "morph" on their wraparound TV screens. On some days he will appear as a nine-year-old runt jacking off in an abandoned grain silo near Texarkana, and on other days he will look like Socrates or Jesus or Abe Lincoln.... But it won't matter, because people will be used to it by then: They will have their own morph-imaging machines, and they will be able to speak directly with the president at least twice a week, on a two-way virtual-reality hookup so real that you can actually "shake hands" with something that looks like the president and "look him in the eye" and squeeze his knuckles until the bones pop wildly back and forth in your grip.

And you will feel it, because you will have VR receptors planted under your skin, and he won't.

THAT IS THE GOOD NEWS.

The bad news is that there will be no year 2000 A.D.—at least not as we know years today—and everything after that will be counted in units of *Hortz*: as in *Hortz 002*, for instance.... The current Gregorian calendar has been obsolete since World War II and no longer serves its purpose.

Not even the Incredible Atomic Clock is accurate any longer. Scientists have been secretly adding "leap seconds" to it for years, hoping against hope that the Earth will somehow right itself.... But *no*. It has been wandering more and more into unpredictable orbits and erratic speeds, and apparently there is no cure for it. The Atomic Clock might run for a very long time, but so will a rat full of speed.... And Speed Kills, like they used to say in Little Rock.

I hate all jokes, as a rule—but every once in a while a good one slips through the cracks, and suddenly you start hearing it on every street corner in America.

Q: Why did the chicken cross the road?

A: To vote for Bill Clinton.

Funny, eh? You bet. Ho, ho....

But not to me, Bubba. When I hear people telling that joke to each other in public, I think they're talking about *me*, and it gives me a queasy feeling.

And I never argue, because it's *true*. Yessir. I crossed that road at high noon in the summer of '92, and I brought a lot of people with me—or at least I tried to, and some people mention it constantly. Even people who once voted for Nixon look down on me now.

But I had my reasons, so fuck them. I would do it again, because I felt it was absolutely necessary to beat George Bush. He was like a rubberized impersonation of Nixon, and I figured Clinton could beat him.

Which was true. We won. Even Bob Dylan went to Washington for the inauguration. *Rolling Stone* called it the Coming of a New Age in American politics. Jack Nicholson stood in the Lincoln Memorial and brought silence to the multitudes by croaking Lincoln's words into a nine-million-watt P.A. system. Young girls went crazy in strange hotel rooms and offered up their virginity to traveling salesmen from Arkansas. Even Thomas Jefferson was said to be happy.

ALMOST EVERYBODY who was anybody went to Washington that week, except me. I had many invitations and far more access than I wanted, along with a penthouse suite at the Embassy Row hotel in the name of Eleanor McGovern—but I went to a sports bar in South San Francisco and watched an NFL football game on TV. It felt like the right thing to do, at the time, and I have never regretted it.

Later I went to the O'Farrell Theatre and watched naked women dance, while discussing Irish politics with my old friend Jim Mitchell.

He seemed hurt that he hadn't received an invitation to the Clinton Inaugural. "You're lucky," I told him. "Wait till you see what happens to the poor bastards who *did* get invited."

In the months that followed I went crazy with grief and fell into a kind of spastic communication with the White House. Life lost all its meaning and I fell into brooding solitude. How had it happened? I wondered. And why to a fine man like me? All I did was vote against George Bush, because he was wrong.

And then I remembered that ancient story about *The Old Woman and the Snake*. It remains my clearest memory of the first time I sat down to lunch with Bill Clinton. I mentioned it at the beginning of the book, and its bears repeating now:

> *An old woman was walking down the road when she saw a gang of thugs beating a poisonous snake. She rescued the snake and carried it back to her home, where she nursed it back to health. They became friends and lived together for many months. One day they were going into town, and the old woman picked the snake up, and it bit her. Repeatedly. "Oh, God," she screamed. "I am dying! Why? I was your friend. I saved your life! I trusted you! Why did you bite me?"*
>
> *The snake looked up at her and said, "Lady, you knew I was a snake when you first picked me up."*

I identified very strongly with the Old Woman—despite hoots and howls from a surprising number of people who said I was obviously the Snake.

When I dealt with Richard Nixon, there was never any question about who was the Old Woman and who was the Snake, and I suspect that is why I got along with him better than I do with Bill Clinton.... Nixon was so aggressively evil that he almost glowed at night. His political instincts were so dangerous that he made the politics of total opposition a very honorable trade for two generations of the best people in America. He gave no mercy and expected none. He was fun.

Clinton is a different kind of animal. He shares Nixon's humble origins and his utterly unprincipled belief in expediency. Nixon was a genuinely paranoid Fatalist who thought *They* were out to get him, and he was right.... We had no choice, really. Richard Nixon was like that 16-wheel Peterbilt in the famous cult movie about a desperate traveling salesman who gets chased across the desert by a kill-crazy semi with no driver. The monster truck pursued him at insane speeds, through phone booths and gas pumps, and even over cliffs, but he never knew *why*.

The difference between Nixon and Clinton is the difference between the Truck and the Traveling Salesman. *The Boss* was our Satan, and Mr. Bill is our Willy Loman. Clinton is "liked, but not *well* liked," and not even his best friends and allies believe anything he says. He has the sense of loyalty of a lizard with its tail broken off and the midnight taste of a man who might go on a double-date with the Rev. Jimmy Swaggart.

Nixon never double-dated. He preferred the three-way: When his future wife, Pat, refused to go to the senior prom with him, he eagerly served as all-night *driver* for the car that carried Pat and her chosen date.

He was weird, Bubba. He played in a league where Clinton will never be anything but a batboy. Nixon was a monster with insanely wrong convictions. Clinton is a humorless punk with bad habits. Nixon was so bad that he could get innocent people *in* to politics, but Clinton is bad in a way that will get all but the worst ones *out*.

WELL...SHUCKS. I guess that's about it for now. These are harsh and terminal judgments that will not be fondly received in the Clinton White House—especially not by a profoundly compromised president who is already running mercilessly for re-election in 1996.... There is no mercy in the Passing Lane, and no place to pull over and park.

Speed kills, they say, and speed is also very addictive. It gets you there faster, and fast is the only way to run if you want to be president of the United States. Buy the ticket, take the ride. Some will march on a road of bones, and others will be nailed up on telephone poles. That is the way it works.

Historians do not call the final ten years of any century "the Decadence" for no reason. It is always a doomed and dissolute time, and the end of the American Century will be no different.... *Generation X* got off easy compared to the hideous fate of the poor bastards in *Generation Z*. They will be like steerage passengers on the *S.S. Titanic*, trapped in the watery bowels of a sinking "unsinkable ship."

It was Ronald Reagan who warned in 1985 that "this generation may be the one that will have to face the end of the world as we know it." There will be no year 2000, except for morphs and pimps and political junkies with no pulse. The president of the United States said that, so we have no reason to doubt it. Good luck.

Memo to Mr. Bill

Don't EVER give up!

Doc H

THE WHITE HOUSE

WASHINGTON

Hunter S. Thompson
Owl Farm
Woody Creek, Colorado 81656

Dear Doc:

Thanks for the drawing you faxed me. I appreciate the inspiration, and I intend to keep working until the last dog dies.

Sincerely,

Bill

Chicago (AP)—April 1, 1994 — Famed author and political journalist Dr. Hunter S. Thompson announced to a cheering crowd of editors, brokers, and elite political professionals in Chicago today that "politics is *not* better than sex" and that he "could not, in good conscience," go ahead with his plan to publish his long-awaited treatise on that subject.

"It is the gibberish of the New Dumb," he said, as the crowd applauded wildly, and "I don't want my name connected with it in any way—especially not in a book that would sit on the shelves of 50,000 libraries for the next 200 years."

Thompson said his publishers "had not been enthusiastic" about his bizarre project from the start, but he had "forced it on them" because of his admitted "addiction to politics" and "extreme personal pressures" from within the Clinton campaign, which he formally endorsed in 1992.

Random House executive editor David Rosenthal said he felt "immensely relieved" that "Hunter has come to his senses" and "can now get back to writing his *real* book—*Polo Is My Life: Memoirs of a Brutal Southern Gentleman,* which will be published in the fall.

"Dr. Thompson can be extremely difficult when he caves in to his political addiction," said Rosenthal. "He has been with us for many years, and we are proud to be his publisher. Hunter is a national treasure and his works will live forever."

PART THREE

NIXON'S THE ONE.

RICHARD MILHOUS NIXON

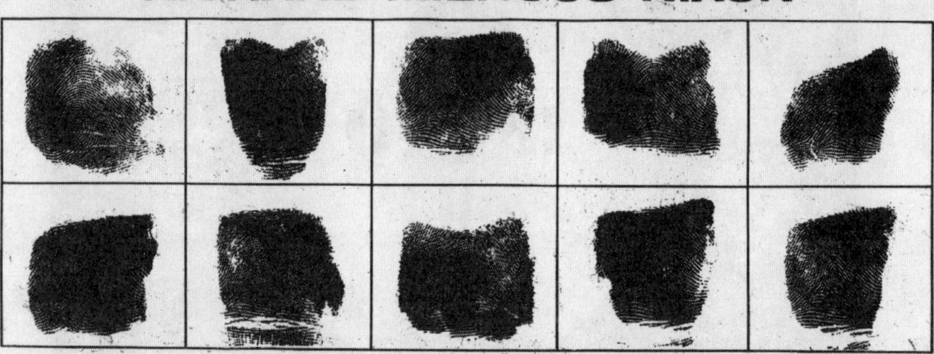

If you have any information concerning this person, please [illegible]ntact the Senate Select Committee Investigating Campaign Activities or Special Prosecutor Co[illegible].

DESCRIPTION

AGE: 60, born January 9, 1913, Yorba Linda, California.

HEIGHT: 5' 11½"	EYES: brown
WEIGHT: 160	COMPLEXION: medium
BUILD: medium	RACE: white
HAIR: brown	NATIONALITY: American

OCCUPATIONS: lawyer; member 80 and 81st Congresses; US senator from California; Vice President of U.S.A.; currently President of U.S.A.

REMARKS: conservative dress, smiles compulsively and gesticulates awkwardly when speaking.

CAUTION

NIXON IS CHARGED WITH THE CONTINUATION AND EXPANSION OF AN ILLEGAL WAR IN SOUTHEAST ASIA, AND CONFESSED TO ORDERING MASSIVE SECRET BOMBING STRIKES IN LAOS AND CAMBODIA. HE HAS REPORTEDLY MISUSED GOVERNMENT AGENCIES TO PERFORM POLITICAL BURGLARIES, BUGGINGS, SPYINGS, AND SABATOGE, AS WELL AS MAINTAINING A SECRET POLICE FORCE TO CONDUCT SUCH COVERT ACTS. ILLEGAL CAMPAIGN TACTICS PERFORMED BY HIS AGENTS AMOUNT TO THEFT OF THE 1972 PRESIDENTIAL ELECTIONS AND NIXON IS CHARGED WITH CONSPIRACY AND OBSTRUCTION OF JUSTICE IN THE WATERGATE SCANDAL. HE IS ALLEGED TO HAVE MADE PERSONAL USE OF PUBLIC FUNDS, MISMANAGED THE NATION'S ECONOMY AND COMMITTED OTHER HIGH CRIMES AND MISDEMEANORS. AT THIS TIME NIXON REMAINS AS CHIEF EXECUTIVE WITH THE FULL POWERS OF THE OFFICE AND IS CONSIDERED DESPERATE AND VERY DANGEROUS.

CHAPTER 666
THE DEATH OF RICHARD NIXON

THE DEATH of Richard Nixon in April 1994 came just as this book was going to press and made it necessary to change the ending. No book about campaign junkies and politics addicts would be complete without including Richard Nixon. He was the ultimate campaign junkie, and his addiction to politics was total. Cheating and lying and stealing were all he really understood in life.

Richard Nixon was the real thing, and I will miss him for the hideous clarity that he brought to my understanding of American politics, and for the anger he inspired in my work. He brought out the best in me, all the way to the end, and for that I am grateful to him. What follows is the obituary that I just delivered to *Rolling Stone*. Read it and weep, for we have lost our Satan. Richard Nixon has gone home to hell.

SPORTS ★ ★ ★ ★ FINAL

DAILY NEWS

40¢ NEW YORK'S HOMETOWN NEWSPAPER Saturday, April 23, 1994

RICHARD M. NIXON

37TH PRESIDENT OF THE UNITED STATES

1913 - 1994

COMPLETE COVERAGE ON PAGES 2 - 8

HE WAS A CROOK

Memo from the National Affairs Desk

Date: May 1, 1994

From: Dr. Hunter S. Thompson

Subject: The Death of Richard Nixon: Notes on the passing of an American Monster...He was a liar and a quitter, and he should have been buried at sea.... But he was, after all, the president.

And he cried mightily with a strong voice, saying, Babylon the great is fallen, and is become the habitation of devils, and the hold of every foul spirit and a cage of every unclean and hateful bird.

—Revelation 18:2

RICHARD NIXON is gone now, and I am poorer for it. He was the real thing—a political monster straight out of Grendel and a very dangerous enemy. He could shake your hand and stab you in the back at the same time. He lied to his friends and betrayed the trust of his family. Not even Gerald Ford, the unhappy ex-president who pardoned Nixon and kept him out of prison, was immune to the evil fallout. Ford, who believes strongly in heaven and hell, has told more than one of his celebrity golf partners that "I know I will go to hell, because I pardoned Richard Nixon."

I have had my own blood relationship with Nixon for many years, but I am not worried about it landing me in hell with him.

I have already been there with that bastard, and I am a better person for it. Nixon had the unique ability to make his enemies seem honorable, and we developed a keen sense of fraternity. Some of my best friends have hated Nixon all their lives. My mother hates Nixon, my son hates Nixon, I hate Nixon, and this hatred has brought us together.

Nixon laughed when I told him this. "Don't worry," he said. "I, too, am a family man, and we feel the same way about you."

IT WAS Richard Nixon who got me into politics, and now that he's gone, I feel lonely. He was a giant in his way. As long as Nixon was politically alive—and he was, all the way to the end—we could always be sure of finding the enemy on the Low Road. There was no need to look anywhere else for the evil bastard. He had the fighting instincts of a badger trapped by hounds. The badger will roll over on its back and emit a smell of death, which confuses the dogs and lures them in for the traditional ripping and tearing action. But it is usually the badger who does the ripping and tearing. It is a beast that fights best on its back: rolling under the throat of the enemy and seizing it by the head with all four claws.

That was Nixon's style—and if you forgot, he would kill you as a lesson to the others. Badgers don't fight fair, Bubba. That's why God made dachshunds.

NIXON WAS a Navy man, and he should have been buried at sea. Many of his friends were seagoing people—Bebe Rebozo, Robert Vesco, William F. Buckley, Jr.—and some of them wanted a full naval burial.

These come is at least two styles, however, and Nixon's immediate family strongly opposed both of them. In the traditionalist style, the dead president's body would be wrapped and sewn loosely in canvas sailcloth and dumped off the stern of a frigate at least 100 miles off the coast and at least 1,000 miles south of San Diego, so the corpse could never wash up on American soil in any recognizable form.

The family opted for cremation until they were advised of the potentially onerous implications of a strictly private, unwitnessed burning of the body of the man who was, after all, the president of the United States. Awkward questions might be raised, dark allusions to Hitler and Rasputin. People would be filing lawsuits to get their hands on the dental charts. Long court battles would be inevitable—some with liberal cranks bitching about corpus delicti and habeas corpus and others with giant insurance companies trying not to pay off on his death benefits. Either way, an orgy of greed and duplicity was sure to follow any public hint that Nixon might have somehow faked his own death or been cryogenically transferred to fascist Chinese interests on the Central Asian Mainland.

It would also play into the hands of those millions of self-stigmatized patriots like me who believe these things already.

If the right people had been in charge of Nixon's funeral, his casket would have been launched into one of those open-sewage canals that empty into the ocean just south of Los Angeles. He was a swine of a man and a jabbering dupe of a president. Nixon was so crooked that he needed servants to help him screw his pants on every morning. Even his funeral was illegal. He was queer in the deepest way. His body should have been burned in a trash bin.

THESE ARE harsh words for a man only recently canonized by President Clinton and my old friend George McGovern—but I have written worse things about Nixon, many times, and the record will show that I kicked him repeatedly long before he went down. I beat him like a mad dog with mange every time I got a chance, and I am proud of it. He was scum.

Let there be no mistake in the history books about that. Richard Nixon was a evil man—evil in every way that only those who believe in the physical reality of the Devil can understand it. He was utterly without ethics or moral or any bedrock sense of decency. Nobody trusted him—except maybe the Stalinist Chinese, and honest historians will remember him mainly as a rat who kept scrambling to get back on the ship.

It is fitting that Richard Nixon's final gesture to the American people was a clearly illegal series of 21 105-mm howitzer blasts that shattered the peace of a residential neighborhood and permanently disturbed many children. Neighbors also complained about another unsanctioned burial in the yard at the old Nixon place, which was brazenly illegal. "It makes the whole neighborhood like a graveyard," said one. "And it fucks up my children's sense of values."

Many were incensed about the howitzers, but they knew there was nothing they could do about it—not with the current president sitting about 50 yards away and laughing at the roar of the cannons. It was Nixon's last war, and he won.

The funeral was a dreary affair, finely staged for TV and shrewdly dominated by ambitious politicians and revisionist historians. The Rev. Billy Graham, still agile and eloquent at the age of 136, was billed as the main speaker, but he was quickly upstaged by two 1996 GOP presidential candidates: Sen. Bob Dole of Kansas, and Gov. Pete Wilson of California, who formally hosted the event and saw his poll numbers crippled when he got blown off the stage by Dole, who somehow seized the number three slot on the roster and uttered such a shameless, self-serving eulogy that even he burst into tears at the end of it.

Dole's stock went up like a rocket and cast him as the early GOP front-runner for '96. Wilson, speaking next, sounded like an Engelbert Humperdink impersonator and probably won't even be reelected as governor of California in November.

The historians were strongly represented by the number two speaker, Henry Kissinger, Nixon's secretary of state and himself a zealous revisionist with many axes to grind. He set the tone for the day with a maudlin and spectacularly self-serving portrait of Nixon as even more saintly than his mother and a president of many godlike accomplishments—most of them put together in secret by Kissinger, who came to California as part of a huge publicity tour for his new book on diplomacy, genius, Stalin, H. P. Lovecraft and other great minds of our time, including himself and Richard Nixon.

Kissinger was only one of the many historians who suddenly came to see Nixon as more than the sum of his many squalid parts. He seemed to be saying that History will not have to absolve Nixon, because he has already done it himself in a massive act of will and crazed arrogance that already ranks him supreme, along with other Nietzschean supermen like Hitler, Jesus, Bismarck and the emperor Hirohito. These revisionists have catapulted Nixon to the status of an American Caesar, claiming that when the definitive history of the 20th century is written, no other president will come close to Nixon in stature. "He will dwarf FDR and Truman," according to one scholar from Duke University.

It was all gibberish, of course. Nixon was no more a Saint than he was a Great President. He was more like Sammy Glick than Winston Churchill. He was a cheap crook and a merciless war criminal who bombed more people to death in Laos and Cambodia than the U. S. Army lost in all of World War II, and he denied it to the day of his death. When students at Kent State University, in Ohio, protested the bombing, he connived to have them attacked and slain by troops from the National Guard.

SOME PEOPLE will say that words like *scum* and *rotten* are wrong for Objective Journalism—which is true, but they miss the point. It was the built-in blind spots of the Objective rules and dogma that allowed Nixon to slither into the White House in the first place. He looked so good on paper that you could almost vote for him sight unseen. He seemed so all-American, so much like Horatio Alger, that he was able to slip through the cracks of Objective Journalism. You had to get Subjective to see Nixon clearly, and the shock of recognition was often painful.

Nixon's meteoric rise from the unemployment line to the vice presidency in six quick years would never have happened if TV had come along 10 years earlier. He got away with his sleazy "my dog Checkers" speech in 1952 because most voters heard it on the radio or read about it in the headlines of their local, Republican newspapers. When Nixon finally had to face the TV cameras for real in the 1960 presidential campaign debates, he got whipped like a redheaded mule. Even die-hard Republican voters were shocked by his cruel and incompetent persona. Interestingly, most people who heard those debates on the radio thought Nixon won. But the mushrooming TV audience saw him as a truthless used-car salesman, and they voted accordingly. It was the first time in 14 years that Nixon lost an election.

When he arrived in the White House as VP at the age of 40, he was a smart young man on the rise—a hubris-crazed monster from the bowels of the American dream with a heart full of hate and an overweening lust to be President. He had won every office he'd run for and stomped like a Nazi on all of his enemies and even some of his friends.

Nixon had no friends except George Will and J. Edgar Hoover (and they both deserted him). It was Hoover's shameless death in 1972 that led directly to Nixon's downfall. He felt helpless and alone with Hoover gone. He no longer had access to either the Director or the Director's ghastly bank of Personal Files on almost everybody in Washington.

Hoover was Nixon's right flank, and when he croaked, Nixon knew how Lee felt when Stonewall Jackson got killed at Chancellorsville. It permanently exposed Lee's flank and led to the disaster at Gettysburg.

For Nixon, the loss of Hoover led inevitably to the disaster of Watergate. It meant hiring a New Director—who turned out to be an unfortunate toady named L. Patrick Gray, who squealed like a pig in hot oil the first time Nixon leaned on him. Gray panicked and fingered White House Counsel John Dean, who refused to take the rap and rolled over, instead, on Nixon, who was trapped like a rat by Dean's relentless, vengeful testimony and went all to pieces right in front of our eyes on TV.

That is Watergate, in a nut, for people with seriously diminished attention spans. The real story is a lot longer and reads like a textbook on human treachery. They were all scum, but only Nixon walked free and lived to clear his name. Or at least that's what Bill Clinton says—and he is, after all, the president of the United States.

Nixon liked to remind people of that. He believed it, and that was why he went down. He was not only a crook but a fool. Two years after he quit, he told a TV journalist that "if the president does it, it can't be illegal."

Shit. Not even Spiro Agnew was that dumb. He was a flat-out, knee-crawling thug with the morals of a weasel on speed.

But he was Nixon's vice president for five years, and he only resigned when he was caught red-handed taking cash bribes across his desk in the White House.

Unlike Nixon, Agnew didn't argue. He quit his job and fled in the night to Baltimore, where he appeared the next morning in U. S. District Court, which allowed him to stay out of prison for bribery and extortion in exchange for a guilty (no contest) plea on income-tax evasion. After that he became a major celebrity and went to work for Coors Beer, where he did odd jobs and played golf. He never spoke to Nixon again and was an unwelcome guest at the funeral. They called him Rude, but he went anyway. It was one of those biological imperatives, like salmon swimming up waterfalls to spawn before they die. He knew he was scum, but it didn't bother him.

Spiro Agnew was the Joey Buttafuoco of the Nixon administration, and J. Edgar Hoover was its Caligula. They were brutal, brain-damaged degenerates worse than any hit man out of *The Godfather*, yet they were the men Richard Nixon trusted most. Together they defined his presidency.

It would be easy to forget and forgive Henry Kissinger of his crimes, just as he forgave Nixon. Yes, we could do that—but it would be wrong. Kissinger is a slippery little devil, a world-class hustler with a thick German accent and a very keen eye for weak spots at the top of the power structure. Nixon was one of these, and Super K exploited him mercilessly, all the way to the end.

Kissinger made the Gang of Four complete: Agnew, Hoover, Kissinger and Nixon. A group photo of these perverts would say all we need to know about the Age of Nixon.

NIXON'S SPIRIT will be with us for the rest of our lives—whether you're me or Bill Clinton or you or Kurt Cobain or Bishop Tutu or Keith Richards or Amy Fisher or Boris Yeltsin's daughter or your fiancee's 16-year-old beer-drunk brother with his braided goatee and his whole life like a thundercloud out in front of him. This is not a generational thing. You don't even have to know who Richard Nixon was to be a victim of his ugly, Nazi spirit.

He has poisoned our water forever. Nixon will be remembered as a classic case of a smart man shitting in his own nest. But he also shit in our nests, and that was the crime that history will burn on his memory like a brand. By disgracing and degrading the presidency of the United States, by fleeing the White House like a diseased cur, Richard Nixon broke the heart of the American Dream.

SEAL OF THE PRESIDENT OF THE UNITED STATES

THE HONOR ROLL

Douglas Brinkley
Stacy Haddash
Will Hearst
Deborah Fuller
Warren Zevon
Juan Thompson
Eleanor McGovern
Ted Yewer
Shelby Sadler
Colleen Gibbons
Gerry Goldstein
Jennifer Winkel
David Rosenthal
Lynn Nesbit
Kurt Papenfus
Richard Nixon
Bill Clinton
Jilly
Doug Carpenter
Tim Ferris

Terry Singh
Bill Greider
Oliver Treibick
Tammy Cimalore
William Burroughs
Tad Floridis
Ed Bradley
Charles Israel
Julie Oppenheimer
Hal Haddon
Catherine Conover
Morris Dees
Chuck Buss
Michael Stepanian
George McGovern
Doris Kearns
Dan Dibble
Gayle Chitty
Rosalyn Carter
Jane Wenner

PHOTO AND ILLUSTRATION CREDITS

Page: iv David Hiser, xi courtesy of *Rolling Stone,* 23 NYT Pictures, 47 Reuters/Bettmann, 63 courtesy of New Hampshire Department of Safety, 70 ©1994 Louie Psihoyos, 101 author's collection, 117 UPI/Bettmann, 146 Reuters/Bettman, 161 courtesy of the LBJ Library Collection, 172 author's collection, 196 AP/Wide World, 236 author's collection, 238 courtesy of the *Daily News,* 247 illustration by Ralph Steadman.

The animals on the following pages were found or derived from the various Dover *Clip-Art* and *Pictorial Archives* Series: xi, xv, 64, 65, 67, 68, 82, 108, 118, 128, 133, 142, 186, 194, 214, 217.

The campaign buttons and ephemera were from the the collection of the author, pages 83, 84, 99, 162, 180; and other private collections, pages 10, 25, 36, 106.